Schubert

Unlocking the Masters Series, No. 19

Schubert

A Survey of His Symphonic, Piano, and Chamber Music

John Bell Young

AMADEUS
PRESS

An Imprint of Hal Leonard Corporation
New York

Published in 2009 by Amadeus Press
An Imprint of Hal Leonard Corporation
7777 West Bluemound Road
Milwaukee, WI 53213

Trade Book Division Editorial Offices
19 West 21st Street, New York, NY 10010

Printed in the United States of America

Book design by Snow Creative Services

Library of Congress Cataloging-in-Publication Data

Young, John Bell.
  Schubert : a survey of his symphonic, piano, and chamber music / by John Bell Young.
    p. cm. – (Unlocking the masters series ; no. 19)
  Includes bibliographical references and index.
  ISBN 978-1-57467-177-3 (alk. paper)
  1. Schubert, Franz, 1797–1828.—Criticism and interpretation. I. Title.

ML410.S3Y78 2009
780.92—dc22
                                                                                    2008045425

www.amadeuspress.com

For Joseph Early and Sandra Rush,

for your support, friendship, and innumerable kindnesses, with love

Contents

Acknowledgments

Writing about music, or any work of art governed by abstraction, is no easy task. One is easily persuaded by force of habit and by long-held beliefs in the veracity of a point of view, as if objectivity were the only thing that mattered.

But as any musicians worth their salt know only too well, there are no ivory towers: music is so complex and abundant as to invite any number of perspectives. And where those perspectives are informed and imaginative, they are worthy of contemplation.

Much the same can be said of any artistic endeavor, and writing is no exception. I am indebted, for their assistance and advice, to a number of friends and colleagues, several of whom did not live to see the completion of this project nor were even aware that what I learned from them would contribute to it so substantially.

Above all there is my late mother, Dorothy Burgess Young, without whose support and unflinching belief in my abilities I could never have written this volume or even so much as played a single note of music.

There are in addition a number of individuals to whom I am indebted for their support and advice, literary and otherwise, while writing this book. First and foremost, I thank my best friend and partner, Michael Vincent Connelly, for his uncompromising friendship, patience, solidarity, tireless assistance, and unwavering faith in my abilities; Joseph Early and Sandra Rush, whose infinite patience, innumerable kindnesses, critical overview, and thoughtful consideration were not only proof of the deepest friendship, but equal to the best editorial advice; Reni Santoni and Tracy Newman, without whose assistance and counsel at a time when I most needed it I would surely never have been able to complete these works; Fred Maroth of Music & Arts Records, who provided many of the exquisite historic recordings; Michael York and Hugh Downs, both experienced authors whose support has been unwavering; Mark and Camilla Tarmy, whose understanding and generosity of spirit know no bounds and who have patiently put up with my sometimes impossible demands for convenience and quietude; Margarita Fyodorova, who taught me all about intonation and much more; Julie Marsden, Greg Brown, Gordon and Emily Jones, and others in the extended Putney School community, for their encouragement, kindness, and help. Finally, thanks to my editor at Amadeus Press, Bernadette Malavarca, and my meticulous copy editor, Angela Buckley.

Finally, to those who are no longer with us, I extend my gratitude in ways that I can only hope will be borne aloft on the wings of angels. From these individuals I learned much of what I know of music. Among them are Constance Keene, a great pianist who was also my teacher and mentor for nearly thirty years; Michel Block, likewise among the great pianists of the twentieth century, whose musical savoir faire and personal gentility were a continual source of knowledge and enrichment; James Landrum Fessenden, a brilliant philosopher and musician whose willingness to share his authoritative knowledge of any number of disciplines, from aesthetics to epistemology and psychoanalysis, has proven invaluable; Norwood and Cornelia Hinkle, whose exemplary years teaching music at the Putney School were an inspiration and who introduced me, as a teenager, to Schubert's chamber music; and both Claudio Arrau and Ernst Levy, the celebrated pianists who, in my few brief encounters with them, taught me more about music making than most could have done in a lifetime.

—*John Bell Young*
Putney, Vermont
June 2008

Introduction

In this volume for Amadeus Press, it is my objective to survey great music from a personal perspective, just as anyone would. Whatever I can convey of my ideas about listening, though informed by analytical scrutiny and historical data, will not be enslaved by technical analysis. While academia continues to do its job in the classroom, pointing out the idiosyncratic formalities of this or that composition as it teaches students to more effectively recognize compositional strategies, I prefer to do what I can to bring music to life in a kind of dialectical dance. This volume, then, is part musical analysis and part interpretation, but above all a personal appreciation. It is not intended to be, nor should it be, construed as a work of scholarship.

Nowhere will I presume that the reader will be following my musical observations, or the accompanying CD, with a score in hand. So often when we listen to music, things seem to fly off the page of the score, or from the hands of the performer, in ways that strike us as inexplicably new and exciting, as if we had just heard the piece for the first time. Perhaps that's just how it should be. In any case, in attempting to put myself in the shoes of listeners, both those who are familiar with this music and those who may not be, I will do my best to bring them into the dynamic fold of the music as it reveals itself. However, this approach will not preclude some harmonic and structural analysis of the music at hand, and, as we shall see, in Schubert's case, this is indispensable. Even so, no one should panic; as there is a great deal to harvest from such magnificent music and, hopefully, from an analysis such as this, which seeks to explore the work from multiple perspectives. And while there are certainly advantages to examining the score, there is also much to be said for letting your ears do what they do best when you trust your instincts: listening!

Though I presume the reader has some knowledge of the vocabulary of music, or access to information that would explain such things as meter, rhythm, note values, bar lines, and the array of Italian-language tempo and dynamic markings, I will nevertheless attempt to demystify some of the larger issues pertaining to musical experience. Furthermore, I have included a glossary of musical terms that will provide readers a heads-up for these concepts.

To this end I will evaluate, describe, and convey as much as possible about compositional process and interpretation. Thus as we begin this survey of Schubert's music, let's have a look at a few basic technical concepts, albeit nothing too intimidating.

Let's start with the notion of *tonality*. What does that really mean? If you think of a work of tonal music—music that depends for its very existence on the organization of its parts into tonal regions, or keys, and their relationships—as a kind of solar system, with planets, asteroids, meteors, light, and space, you will also have to conclude that somewhere or other there lurks a sun, too. And just about everything in this musically configured solar system orbits around that sun.

What I am getting at here is that the home key is akin to the sun, and its purpose similar. The home (tonic) key is a kind of sonorous landscape that gives sanctuary to all the parts of a composition and welcomes them home after they drift away or go off on their own into other keys. This tonal center exerts its own kind of gravitational pull, too. Everything in its sphere of influence moves inexorably toward it, and we experience this movement as fulfilling. The moment we return to the home key we sense a certain satisfaction, as if things were meant to return there all along. In turn, the parts of the composition—its rhythmically organized notes and motives—are irradiated by the heat of this musical sun, which not only envelops its progeny in its ever-present rays, but assures them of its power and permanence.

If I may digress for a moment, I would like to propose changing the paradigm for the discussion and analysis of music. For those who may not be so comfortable with technical terminology, whether it be fundamental or arcane, have no fear: while I could certainly refer to the home key of any tonal composition as the *tonic*, or to its closest relations as the *dominant*, *subdominant*, and *mediant* (the common terminology of harmonic analysis), I prefer, for the purposes of this book, to deal with less technical matters and instead to raise more experiential questions: How is it possible for our ears recognize a musical event as it happens in real time, and once we do, how do we determine its significance? Are some events more significant than others? And while it's all well and good to identify the various elements of a musical composition by name, what use is that kind of exercise for listeners who are unable to do so?

To appreciate and recognize significant compositional events as they occur, it may prove more productive to focus our attention on the rhythmic and melodic progression of the work at hand. In other words, what we ought to ask ourselves as listeners is not to which key this or that chord belongs, or how the imposition of a Schenker graph would illuminate both form and harmonic structure, but something even more essential: where are things—by which I mean melodies and rhythms—going, where did they come from in the first place, and how did they get there? By what visceral or aural means can listeners untrained in the vocabulary and complexes of music find their way home and back?

Think of it this way: all of us know very well our own home. We know how it is laid out, where the furniture is, where we've made open space or indifferently created clutter. If we are particularly well organized, we may even know what lurks in the darkest recesses of every closet and behind the rakes and shovels in the garage. During a power failure, when everything is thrown into total darkness, we can find our way around, though the gentle illumination of a small candle, even in a familiar place, would be welcome and could prevent us from stumbling over the unforeseen.

If this sounds like the stuff of an Alfred Hitchcock thriller, it is indeed possible to make an analogy to the genre of the mystery novel. Just as Agatha Christie keeps us on our toes in anticipation of whodunit, providing clues alluded to by the heroes and villains of her texts, so does a composer proffer information, albeit in musical categories. These musical clues are called *motives*, which are the musical equivalent to literary characters.

We can easily recognize a motive, no matter how brief, by its rhythm, pitch organization, melody, or mood. The eminently familiar first four notes of Beethoven's Fifth Symphony, for example, form the driving motive of that work. All great composers are resourceful, never failing to organize the elements of their music clearly and intelligibly so as to allow us to follow their train of thought. They will provide signposts and goals, and as the work progresses, they will develop, vary, and elaborate their materials. Eventually the home key—our sun—will reappear on the compositional horizon and beckon us back to the familiar place where the journey began.

With the reader's indulgence, this is a good place to take a step back to examine yet another important dimension of musical composition. The prolongation of a single pitch is called a *pedal point*. Pedal points enhance our experience of the synaptic connections— the space that occurs between any two notes—that link one tone to another. This is because pedal points create a kind of background, or frame, against which we can more easily discern how the pitch material surrounding them, and which they modify, evolves. Indeed, the continual drone of a single pitch or pitches within the context of a busier contrapuntal fabric is not without purpose; ironically, though the prolongation of a single tone might at first appear to be a mechanism for establishing harmonic or rhythmic stability, the net effect is just the opposite: as pedal points linger in a perpetual background buzz, what is created is tension, uncertainty, and anxiety.

But the effect is nevertheless palpable. Pedal points await resolution not only from within the music itself, but also in relation to our listening habits. Consciously or not, we expect pedal points to dissolve themselves and relieve the tension they have engendered and in which have embroiled our expectations. That they do not always do so, thus frustrating our expectations, serves only to create greater musical tension. The unruffled, even dominating presence of pedal points demands our attention, as they heighten our aural expectations in anticipation of their idiosyncratic destiny.

Savvy listeners will strive to cultivate their listening habits and inscribe themselves within the musical activity, as if they are themselves creating the music as it unfolds in time. To a certain extent listeners, as real-time participants who process the stream of sound, are doing just that. In art music, complexity—that is, the myriad parts, rhythms, harmonies, and, not least, the relationships that each of these has to the other—is something not to be feared, but to be embraced. Listeners who are untrained in analysis and find themselves unable to name this or that compositional form, harmony, or technical particle should not be intimidated. Not everyone is a professional musician, or can be, and woe be unto a society replete with professionals but wanting for amateurs. In the final analysis, having an encyclopedic knowledge of music in all its details is unnecessary and unimportant for the nonprofessional music lover, because when it gets right down to it, what really matters is listening with an open mind and an open heart.

To this end we can, each and every one of us, decipher musical form, whether in its smallest incarnation (the motive), which is nothing more than a fragment of a larger picture, or in its largest array, be it a fugue or a sonata. Repetition is vital to understanding the architecture of musical form. Thus it is not without purpose, both structural and pragmatic, that the laws of composition have traditionally demanded the repetition of whole sections. As we listen to music, doing our best to follow its myriad melodies, fascinating rhythms, and changing harmonies, patterns emerge. These patterns embed themselves in our perception and memory. It is to these patterns that our ears become accustomed. Through this process, with the composer's help, the destiny of each motive evolves before our eyes (or, should I say, our ears) and catches fire on form, to cite the German philosopher and music critic Theodor W. Adorno. Finally, a motive takes its place within the larger formal context it informs, influences, and ultimately helps to create.

The current volume concerns the music of Schubert, who composed more than a thousand pieces of music, more than six hundred of them lieder. If only it were possible to write about each and every one of his compositions in this modest volume, I would, but alas, it is not. Nor is it desirable; a critique requires more than sound bites, and to enter into a serious discussion of so much music would demand several thick volumes, not one. Instead, I've taken a look at a representative swath of his major symphonic, chamber, and piano music. Admittedly, these few works number among my favorites and are likewise well established and often performed staples of the repertoire; the reader is likely to encounter them often in concert and on disc. By illuminating their content, I hope to provide the reader with a renewed appreciation of Schubert's remarkably original and even opulent music. For those interested in a substantive discussion of Schubert's lieder, I recommend *Schubert's Theater of Song*, by Mark Ringer, which is likewise published by Amadeus Press in the Unlocking the Masters series.

Where a discussion of technical matters is concerned, particularly key relationships, Schubert is a special case and presents unique challenges. To survey even one of his major compositions without exploring his ingenious use of migrating key centers would be ill-advised and probably pointless. Thus to a limited extent I have resolved to examine these issues as best I can throughout this book.

The accompanying glossary provides succinct definitions of theoretical terminology. To help simplify this analysis, just think of each of the musical terms as representing a significant change or event of some sort: invariably, such changes and events refer to harmony, rhythm, dynamics, and melody.

Music is an adventure. If I am successful in cultivating in readers a renewed curiosity about its many recesses and shadows, rivulets and canyons, all the better. Certainly I make no claims to be right or wrong. The most rigorous harmonic and formal analyses are probably better taken up by theorists and scholars, whose work is more useful to each other than to nonexpert music lovers. The latter, after all, are those who simply strive to become as intimate with musical experience as they can without becoming scientists. I dedicate this volume to those *amateurs de la musique*, and I hope they will find within its pages something of value.

Schubert

Franz Schubert:
An Overview

Franz Peter Schubert was no Blanche DuBois; he relied on the kindness of friends, not strangers. Were it not for that fact, Schubert's innate modesty might only have served to smother his brief career. Here was a man, after all, whose gifts, though titanic, were overshadowed in his lifetime by Beethoven's. Here was a composer who, despite his limitless potential, was dutifully marginalized by the far more popular and well-heeled Carl Maria von Weber. And here was a young man, always eager to please, who settled pretty much for whatever came his way.

Though Schubert did not revile success or abandoned whatever dreams he may have harbored for it, the fact remains that he was neither a fighter nor confrontational. He never allowed his ego to rule his ambitions, any more than he allowed vanity to interfere with his creative process. He was, if anything, preternaturally shy. This timorousness compromised his material (but not musical) ambitions. Skeptical publishers, unwilling to take a chance on a composer barely out of his teens as the second decade of the nineteenth century came to a close, more often than not rejected his submissions. And though he may have expressed his frustration and disappointment to friends, he never argued with the powers that be nor stood up in his own defense. It simply wasn't in his character to do so. As we shall see, there were other, perhaps more illuminative reasons for the relatively meager reception his music garnered, at least when he was alive. Not the least of these was a general lack of aristocratic patronage, such as Haydn, Mozart, Beethoven, and others enjoyed, which had long been a traditional and immensely valuable asset to the career of any burgeoning composer.

That Beethoven ruled musical Europe while the young Schubert was trying to make his way was only a happy coincidence; Schubert idolized the older composer, and though he yearned to know him, and perhaps to study with him, he was too shy to do either. Even here his shyness compromised his ambition, which was in any case less concerned with material gain that with artistic accomplishment. If that outlook proved naive and cost him valuable opportunities in his lifetime—opportunities to have his music published and widely distributed, for example—it did nothing to rob him posthumously of the credit he deserved. Fortunately for posterity, his music, for all its Apollonian beauty and originality, transcended the personal circumstance of his life. Had his work, on the other hand, merely vanished into obscurity, that alone would have said a great deal more about his person and his talent than any biography. Indeed, his music survived, not simply because of its abundant charming melodies and pristine construction, but because it spoke so eloquently to the human condition.

Even so, the romantic, even Bohemian dimensions of his life had other, perhaps less favorable consequences for his reputation, musically and otherwise. Indeed, for more than a century after his death in 1828, a litany of apocryphal myths, inspired by his presumably Bohemian lifestyle, infested both the popular imagination and critical evaluation. It seems that no one was safe from the aura in which Franz Schubert was sanctified or, more accurately, reified. One fanciful myth after the other sprang up in the decades after his death, making of his life something akin to tabloid fodder. I do not refer to stories of his sexual orientation, which Maynard Solomon and other scholars have persuasively demonstrated (but not definitively proved) was that of a gay man. Nor do I challenge the debate as to the cause of his death, which was likely typhoid fever (mercury poisoning has likewise been blamed for bringing about his early demise) but could also have been syphilis, a disease that he battled valiantly for the last six years of his life. To avoid the issue of sex, any number of early biographies and papers ignored or didn't even bother to mention his syphilis, thus rendering Schubert something on the order of a saint while making his life story more palatable for prudent masses. In any case, these biographical data are not myths, but fact, or, in the case of his homosexuality, for which there is compelling evidence, likely fact.

The myths to which I refer concern Schubert's contemporary reputation as a composer and his overall material well-being. As the current volume is neither biography nor psychoanalytic exegesis, any substantive discussion of these issues is neither germane nor even relevant to the music itself, which is the object of this study. Even so, there may be some value in exploding a few popular myths right off the bat, as sentimentality or pity has no role, nor should it play one, in the objective, or even the subjective evaluation of his music.

Anecdotes and legends, drawn from the elaborate picaresque hearsay of Schubert's friends, acquaintances, and early biographers, have long flourished, leading classical-music neophytes to mistake myth for fact. Poor Schubert, as he has been so often called (in consequence of a few letters in which he referred to himself that way out of modesty, not in reference to his financial health), has alternately been feminized, demeaned as a homeless indigent who was incapable of finding a publisher, and characterized as a composer who was so widely ignored by the press and public of his era that he nearly starved to death.

None of that is true, though it made for an appealing human-interest story that sold books and magazines. It did just that in Rudolf Hans Bartsch's sentimental 1912 novel *Schwammerl* (The Little Mushroom), which was the pet name that Schubert's friends affectionately anointed him with), a frivolous literary confection that reinvented Schubert as a jolly but luckless Bohemian male spinster. A few years later, a minor composer, Heinrich Berthe, inspired by *Schwammerl*'s popularity, went on to compose one of the most successful operettas of all time, *Das Dreimäderlhaus*, which served to perpetuate the notion of Schubert as a carefree, happy-go-lucky dilettante who wrote pleasant country dances and innocuous songs.

The fundamental facts about his life are well known. He was born on January 31, 1797, in Himmelpfortgrund, population three thousand, in the Vienna suburb of Liechtental district. His father, Franz Theodor Florian Schubert, was a schoolmaster, and his mother, Maria Elisabeth Katharina Vietz, had been a cook, up until the time of her marriage, in a prosperous Viennese household. The Schuberts had fourteen children, only five of whom survived their young years. When Schubert was fifteen, his mother came down with typhoid fever, as he would himself years later, and died. Schubert's musical training began in earnest when he was barely five years old. His father, an amateur musician, taught his son to play the violin, while his tutelage in piano became the responsibility of his older brother, Ignaz. Around the same time, he was entrusted to one Michael Holzer, an organist at the Liechtenthal Parish Church, where he received additional instruction on the keyboard. The Schuberts routinely held private performances in their home. The prodigious Schubert was barely fourteen when he composed his first string quartets.

In the year 1808, Schubert matriculated at the Vienna Stadtkonvikt, a boarding school and choir college for the children of the bourgeoisie and working class. Simultaneously, he gained admittance to the choirs of two particularly prestigious institutions, the Imperial Court Chapel and Royal Seminary, where he sang his heart out as a boy soprano. But it was at the Stadtkonvikt that he studied composition with Antonio Salieri, the celebrated Italian composer and rival of Mozart. True to form, the curmudgeonly Salieri tried to persuade the young Schubert to give up his dream of composing lieder, which did not befit the aspirations, in the establishment's view, of any serious composer.

Leaving the Stadtkonvikt in 1813, Schubert went on to study at St Anna Teachers' Training College in Vienna, with a view toward becoming a teacher, like his father. Indeed, a year later he accepted his father's offer to join him as an assistant at his school in Himmelpfortgrund, where he was assigned the supervision of six-year-olds. It was a job toward which he was ill disposed and even more ill suited. His fascination with the poetry of Schiller, Goethe, and Klopstock, and his determination to set it to music, annoyed his father, who was indignant at his son's refusal to pursue *real* work. Nevertheless, by 1814, Schubert had begun to set the first of seventy of Goethe's poems to music, resulting in his first bona-fide masterpiece, *Gretchen am Spinnrade*; just a year later, he composed "Erlkönig," which would later become the anthem of his fleeting, and then posthumous, fame.

He was barely nineteen when he quit his job at his father's school and left the bosom of his family. He hadn't been getting on well with his father for some time, their once pleasant father–son banter now frequently erupting into raucous argument. He chose to share digs with his free-spirited, hedonistic friend Franz von Schober in Vienna. This was hardly an unusual arrangement in those days, especially for a young person in search of stability. But despite the rift with his father, and the absence of a regular income, to say that he was impoverished is an exaggeration. Though it is perhaps technically feasible to surmise as much, at least in statistical categories, the fact remains that his quality of life was comfortable. He was well cared for and wanted for nothing, save extravagance; when he did have money, he squandered it liberally. What's more, his middle-class origins and enlightened education ensured him access to a reasonably well-heeled circles. Additionally, the ongoing support and patronage of his closest friends, many of whom he met at school and who believed in his potential, assured him a roof over his head and food on his table.

Soon enough, though, Schubert's reputation began to spread, thanks in part to numerous musicales at his family home and, later, at the homes of his friends and patrons. Each of these concerts became a private showcase for his music. In the three-year period from 1814 to 1817, the sheer volume of his compositional output was astonishing; in that brief time he composed no fewer than three hundred songs, five symphonies, four masses, six operas, and at least three piano sonatas. Virtually none of these, save for a handful of the songs, was performed publicly or published.

Following the debut in 1821 of "Erlkönig," which became his most popular lied, things began to turn around, albeit slowly. Certainly, Schubert was fortunate to have engaged for that debut a celebrated singer, Johann Michael Vogl, who became one of his most ardent protagonists, as well as an old friend, the composer and pianist Anselm Huttenbrenner. This concert became the first major, germinal event in his career and brought him to the attention of publishers and music lovers beyond Austrian borders. In the same year he was diagnosed and hospitalized with syphilis, he set to work on the "Unfinished" Symphony in B Minor, a singspiel called *Die Verschworenen* (which one might glibly characterize as the nineteenth-century version of an American musical), and an opera, *Fierrabras*. Unhappily, the opera was a critical failure; although the vocal writing is no less meticulous than that of his songs, and the music fascinates for its harmonic orientation, the theatrical and dramatic dimensions in which these ought to coalesce, as they would in a great opera, were woefully inadequate.

Despite the opera's disappointing reception, Schubert's income from performances, publications, dedications, teaching, and patronage increased, yielding him a modest but respectable financial footing. Indeed, the notion that only a few of the more than one thousand works he composed were ever published in his lifetime is rubbish; the fact is that a great deal of his music saw the light of day after 1821, even if much of that repertoire was his vocal music. Ironically, it was precisely this success with lieder that may have served to compromise his fame even further. Until Schubert came along, the song (or *lied*) did not hold much currency among the serious-minded. Though it enjoyed as a genre and had a certain popularity with the public, critics and music theorists of the day did not exactly hold the lied in the highest esteem, convinced that it could never equal in substance or potential either symphonic or operatic music. Indeed, the art song was widely viewed as an essentially amateur confection, the entire purpose of which was to showcase the talent of its performer. Thus, those in the know marginalized its currency as a legitimate aesthetic product. Even Goethe, the greatest poet of the age, demurred when approached by Schubert's friend Josef von Spaun, who proposed the publication of eight volumes of songs, each and every one set to Goethe's poetry. When offered a fresh copy of "Erlkönig," one of Schubert's greatest masterworks and likewise set to his poem, Goethe didn't even bother to respond.

Regardless of the esteem his lieder would bring him post-mortem, Schubert was viewed, in the years immediately following his death, as a composer of charming songs and incidental music. Given that he composed more than six hundred songs, it's no wonder. Never mind his prodigious productivity: this view of Schubert as something less than a great composer is obvious from the epitaph that his friend the poet and playwright Franz Grillparzer had embedded in the architrave atop his tomb: "The art of music here interred a rich possession. But far fairer hopes still." Grillparzer's tribute, while well intentioned, sums up the party line of the musical establishment in 1828: that Schubert never reached his artistic potential. Well, what they didn't know certainly won't hurt them now.

Of course, it's hard to blame his contemporaries for this attitude. After all, his symphonic output and mature piano music was largely unknown and rarely published in his lifetime; nor was it performed, save for a few read-throughs that proved inconsequential to his career and reputation. Some, but hardly all, of his piano and chamber music saw the light of day, was published, and was occasionally championed by professional concert artists of his acquaintance. Indeed, it was decades before the great C Major String Quintet, for example, was afforded its premiere, and the first performance of the Unfinished Symphony took place in 1863.

It was de rigueur in Schubert's day for any composer worth his salt to write symphonies and operas and to have these published and performed. This sort of musical pedigree was indispensable to material gain—that is, for a composer's financial independence, influence, and, in the rare cases, celebrity. Schubert had penned works in both genres, but in the absence of their performance and publication, the chances of achieving either diminished substantially. His symphonies were never performed in his lifetime, and his operas *Fierrabras* and *Alfonso und Estrella* foundered, largely because of the internecine intrigue within the theaters that commissioned them. Whereas Beethoven, already world famous, had long been the darling of the press and public, enjoying widespread publication and distribution of his works, Schubert was at odds with the business of music as he competed for its attention.

It certainly didn't help matters that Schubert was neither a virtuoso pianist nor a first-class string player; his ability to perform his own music limited his prospects with both the public and the print media. He never honed his instrumental talents to a degree that, like Mozart and Beethoven, would have stimulated the public to learn more about him. That he commanded a pleasant singing voice was not enough to satisfy the vitally important publishing industry, which measured the public's interest in anything and everything new. However, it would be inaccurate to say that he had no interest or avoided the promotion of his music; on the contrary, he was tireless in his zeal to put his music at the disposal of his friends, colleagues, and supporters whenever possible, with the hope of having it reach a wider audience.

Thus, a career as a concert artist, which would likely have brought Schubert the level of celebrity he coveted, was lost to him. Absent the benefits that virtuosity would have afforded him—notoriety, travel, artistic ubiquity, and, most important, greater access to and clout with established music publishers—he labored at a disadvantage. No matter how remarkable his musical output, no matter how ingenious the products of his imagination, publishers dared not take on too much of it, at least until he was able to prove to their satisfaction that he could spread his wings and win, like Beethoven, the overall affection of the public. Without the active participation of the composer, who was expected to proselytize on behalf of his own artistic inventiveness as he wowed audiences across the Continent, the business of music could only hedge its bets. Schubert was a risky investment while he was alive.

Schubert's professional fortunes might have improved considerably had he lived even one more year. In March 1828, a year to the day of Beethoven's death, and only months before Schubert's own demise, friends and supporters organized a concert of his music in Vienna. It was a smashing success, critically and financially, and publishers from abroad, mostly northern Germany, came calling. Among them were B. Schott and Sons and Heinrich Albert Probst, whose firm in Leipzig ranked among the most prestigious in Europe. Schubert offered them a number of his most recent works, including the E-flat Piano Trio, D. 929, the F Minor Fantasy for Piano Four Hands, D. 940, and the Four Impromptus, Op. 90 (or D. 899). Even then, his negotiations with publishers dissolved into tedium, and publication was delayed until well after his death.

From a twenty-first-century perspective, Schubert's decidedly uncompetitive persona seems hard to reconcile, especially in light of his temporal, geographical and artistic proximity to such celebrated musical figures as Beethoven, Chopin, and Weber. A more prolific worker would be hard to imagine; indeed, in his all-too-brief career he composed more than a thousand works, not the least of which were the six hundred lieder, various chamber music, the seven completed symphonies, two operas, masses, an oratorio (*Lazarus*), and numerous piano works. Certainly, his reputation as one of the greatest composers in the history of Western civilization has survived him admirably. But how could that be, given the overall lack of interest in his work during his lifetime?

Well, the answer lies in the power and inventiveness of the music itself, which went on to enjoy a life of its own. But on a more pragmatic note, Schubert himself, by virtue of his retiring behavior, modesty, and kindness, was more than a little responsible for the fate of his compositional progeny. In a world entirely devoid of electronics, instant communication, and mass media, even the most brilliant and well-heeled were pretty much on their own. Travel was difficult, time-consuming, expensive, and even dangerous in a hierarchical society where everyone was expected to conform. Indeed, in early nineteenth-century Vienna, where Schubert lived and died, the secret police were everywhere. Conformity meant invisibility, and invisibility meant safety. In the competitive world of music, and in light of what society demanded of its artists, Schubert, who likely intuited the ultimate value and humanity of his work, resolved to play things safe. A prima donna he was not. His musical compositions were his children, and just as any parent would, he sacrificed the pleasures of everyday life to ensure their future safety. Whether this was a deliberate strategy or merely instinctive is anyone's guess, but the abundant goodwill he generated both as a man and as a musician served him well for the next two hundred years and continues to do so to this day.

The years 1827 and 1828, which saw the election of Andrew Jackson as president of the United States, the first publication of Webster's Dictionary, the invention of the common match, and a catastrophic typhoon that nearly decimated Japan, were a productive time for Schubert. In that brief window, he composed three extraordinary and interrelated Piano Sonatas (in C Minor, D. 958; A Major, D. 959; and B-flat Major, D. 960), which proved to be his last effort in the genre; two sets of Impromptus, D. 899 and D. 935; the great song cycle *Winterreise*, D. 911; the songs of the *Schwanengesang* (Swan Song, D. 957), the beginnings of a tenth symphony (which he never finished);

the Piano Trios in B-flat Major, D. 898; and E-flat Major, D. 929; and the Mass in E-flat, D. 950). His health deteriorated rapidly, as his body was ravaged by syphilis and most likely typhoid fever. These illnesses left him virtually immobile by late autumn. He devoted time to reading the work of James Fenimore Cooper, which inspired him. No longer able to withstand the pain, his fragile body gave out, and he died on November 19, 1828, at the age of thirty-one.

In the years after his death, a number of famous musicians, not the least of whom were Felix Mendelssohn and Johannes Brahms, took up Schubert's cause, using their clout to make certain his music was performed, studied, and distributed. Better late than never. Robert Schumann in particular carried the torch, becoming Schubert's chief propagandist in numerous articles he wrote for the *Neue Zeitschrift für Musik*. It was Schumann who, in referring to the Ninth Symphony, coined the term "heavenly length," which, for good or bad, has attached itself to Schubert's music for the better part of the last 280 years. Even George Grove, the founder of Grove's Dictionary, and the British composer Sir Arthur Sullivan (of *Gilbert and Sullivan* fame) made a sojourn in 1867 to Vienna, where they acquired manuscripts of seven of Schubert's symphonies, several operas and masses, numerous chamber pieces, and the incidental music to *Rosamunde*.

And what of Schubert's music? What makes it so unique? While it would be easy enough to talk about its sumptuous melodies, its harmonic inventiveness that extols the virtues of migrating tonalities, its seductive power and humbling simplicity, there is something else about it that moves and moves in on its listeners: its affective intensity. There is something psychedelic about Schubert's sound world, with its bounty of unexpected harmonies, its crystalline counterpoint, its effervescent melodies, and its lively rhythm, all of which, no matter how complex, remain fluid. And while the idea of psychedelia may seem historically inappropriate to the music of the late classical or early romantic eras, it rings true to the ear. There is a magical quality about Schubert's music, especially the mature works after 1820, that speaks to us in a tongue of mercurial fantasy. Its melancholy voice, now manic, now wistful, is at once elusive and endearing.

The Symphonies (Nos. 4, 5, 8, and 9)

The number of symphonies Schubert composed in his brief career has long been a matter of some confusion, among the public and among scholars. The fault is not entirely his but lies with his devotees and also arises from differences of perception and opinion among his cataloguers.

Schubert composed seven complete symphonies, not including the Seventh, D. 729 (which, as we shall see, existed only as a sketch) or the Eighth (the "Unfinished," D. 759), the latter of which, although it is a fully mature and integrally complete work, contains only two movements. Even so, to refer to the "Unfinished" Symphony as merely a torso is merely a truism and essentially irrelevant, even though Schubert left behind piano sketches for a Scherzo movement.

In 1821 Schubert fleshed out his officially designated Seventh Symphony in E Major, in a more substantive way, orchestrating the first 110 bars of the introduction to the first movement and providing the melodic design, bass line, and instructions for orchestration for its remainder. Despite that groundwork, the Seventh Symphony remains incomplete. What is occasionally performed today as Schubert's Seventh is any one of several speculative completions drawn by composer-scholars, who, no matter how sincere, gifted, informed, and distinguished in their own right, have crafted entirely new and autonomous edifices that, for all the ingenuity invested in them, are not Schubert. This is not to suggest that such efforts are unworthy; on the contrary, even works of this variety, which might more properly be labeled transcriptions, compel our attention and serve to reveal something about Schubert's aesthetic agenda at a particularly significant period of his life.

Schubert was barely sixteen when he composed his First Symphony in D Major, Op. 82, and he went on to write five more over the next five years. Certainly, the rate of production was astounding, but more compelling still is the authority of his craftsmanship. While Mozart and Beethoven loomed nearby, and his enthusiastic admiration of their work was well known, he never settled for mere imitation. Even at his tender age, he already commanded the compositional vocabulary of classicism: period phrasing, sonata and rondo form, rustic sforzandos, brilliant scales, bucolic trios with rustic horn calls and triadic configurations, audacious scherzos, virulent crescendos, and gradual diminuendos had all become as familiar to him as old friends. His burgeoning harmonic palette, which would take only a few years to develop into something exceptionally rich and individual, effortlessly accounted for the tense relationship between chromatic colorations and secondary dominants.

Schubert's sketches for a tenth symphony materialized after his death. And like the Seventh, composer-scholars have issued speculative completions of it. For the purposes of this book I've resolved that time would be best spent in taking a look at music that Schubert, and Schubert alone, composed. To this end I have selected four of his symphonies, including the "Unfinished."

Symphony No. 4 in C Minor, D. 417 ("The Tragic")

*Violins 1 and 2; violas; cellos; 2 flutes; 2 oboes; 2 clarinets in
    B-flat; 2 bassoons; 4 horns in A, C, and E-flat; 2 trumpets in
    C and E-flat; timpani*
Completed in 1816

First movement: Adagio molto—Allegro vivace
Second movement: Andante
Third movement: Menuetto—Allegretto vivace
Fourth movement: Allegro

On the heels of "Erlkönig," the centerpiece of his short-lived celebrity, Schubert penned this, his Fourth Symphony in B-flat Major. Jane Austen had just written her audacious novel *Emma*, which titillated readers, while in far-off America, James Monroe celebrated his election as the fifth president of the United States. Meanwhile, in Schubert's hometown, Vienna, the German-born Beethoven had already completed his nature-inspired Sonata No. 28 in D Major, the so-called "Pastorale," not to be confused with his Sixth Symphony, which bore the same title.

Though barely nineteen years old, Schubert had already written the chilling lied "Erlkönig" a year earlier, in 1815. While it went on to become his musical calling card following its public premiere six years later and won widespread recognition as a milestone in the history of the vocal literature, his efforts in the symphonic genre continued to languish, at least critically. As we have already observed, and student read-throughs at Konvikt of his earliest efforts in the genre notwithstanding, not one of his symphonies was performed publicly in his lifetime, including this one.

Oddly enough, while his gift for song was Olympian, their melodies and psychological nuances pouring out of him ready-made like so much holy water, his orchestral inventions sprung from labor and derivative invention. His first three outings in the genre yielded charming, frothy confections that were well suited to the student ensembles that read through them at Konvikt. But with the "Tragic" Symphony, his powers as a symphonist began to bloom in earnest.

It's no secret, either, that for Schubert, the composition of the Fourth Symphony represented something else: a passion and hope for success, not only artistically but materially. When he set to work on the score in 1816, he had already been in the employ of his taskmaster father, gaining what was doubtless valuable experience as an assistant teacher at Himmelpfortgrund. And though he put up with the work's quotidian demands and the mediocrities of his students—who were barely younger than him—he never seems to have complained. Even so, we can only imagine the enthusiasm he savored for himself in writing this symphony, which marked, in a very real sense, the culmination of his powers as a symphonist; here his talent came into its own, his voice blossoming into the auburn beginnings of the Schubert the whole world would not-so-soon thereafter come to know and love. It was a moment he had prepared for, studiously, with conviction. That nothing was to come of it materially or critically does not matter, even if it failed to gain attention, much less a performance in his lifetime. Indeed, the efficacy and substance of what is now viewed as his first important work in the genre adumbrated even greater things and contributed to an imagination so vivid and abundant that it would influence virtually everything he wrote for the next for the next twelve years, that is, to the end of his life. After all, Beethoven was thirty years old before he wrote his own First Symphony and had its premiere in Vienna, whereas Schubert, barely out of his teens, had already penned four.

There is nothing particularly tragic about the "Tragic" Symphony, though the moniker is one that Schubert himself attached to it, for reasons that remain undiscerned. Certainly, its temporal proximity to his composition of the truly tragic ambience of the "Erlkönig" might have had something to do with it; or perhaps his having failed to win an appointment, around the same time, as a music teacher at a school in Laibach (which on today's map is the city of Ljubljana in Slovenia) led to a disposition wherein disappointment, as it so often does with teenagers, morphed into tragedy. Or perhaps his quiet dissatisfaction and overall reluctance as a dutiful son serving his father's interests as an assistant led him to see himself in a tragic position.

Not least, of course, as Schubert scholar Charles Fisk has shrewdly brought to everyone's attention, is the complex relationship, which may well have been redolent with unspoken hostility, between the young Schubert and his father, from whom he felt estranged, or at least—and to put it more gently—who he felt to be a stranger to his sensibility. Indeed, in contradiction to the customary party line that Schubert had no literary aspirations of his own, that is, as a writer of poetry or prose, an unpublished fictional story in his own hand, *Mein Traum* (My Dream), discovered among his papers after his death, suggests otherwise.

Many major composers of the nineteenth century fancied themselves to be wordsmiths, philosophers, and writers; Liszt, Berlioz, Schumann, and Wagner, to name the most prolific, considered their literary efforts as nearly equal in importance to their musical output. Schubert declined to pursue any such sideline, but that he tried his hand at it is significant. The protagonist of *Mein Traum* is a young boy who, twice banished by his own father following arguments (over food and merriment), sets off to discover himself and the world. His only refuge, during his journey, is song, and in song he enshrouds himself, before succumbing to the charms of a mystical circle of older men—a fantasy that sounds curiously similar to what one would find at a Masonic Temple—who he finds gathered at the grave of a dead virgin. Here, the protagonist finds redemption and forgiveness, not only for himself, but for his father, as well. As for the virgin (or maiden), she may well have represented the protagonist, and thus Schubert's musical aspirations. She may also have represented Schubert's mother, who died only a few years before the completion of the "Tragic" Symphony. Nor is it insignificant that in the year 1816 Schubert became infatuated, perhaps romantically, with the singer Terese Grob, for whom he wrote a number of songs and solos in his early Mass. In the household of dream analysis, the very name Grob can indicates a play on words, since in German, *Grab* means "grave."

That this is the first of his symphonic works in a minor key lends a certain gravitas, too, to the idea of the tragic. Even so, Schubert did not append the tragic moniker to this work until some time after he finished it, thus suggesting that the entire notion was a kind of afterthought. A cynical spin might attribute his decision to ambition, and a desire for recognition in the popular marketplace. In any case, the Fourth Symphony, as it emerges, has less in common with the rough-and-tumble declamations of Beethoven's Fifth, but shares an ideology of intent with the Sturm und Drang movement (in music as well as literature) that influenced the waning years of the preceding century. It is nothing if not portentous and at times onomatopoetic; its expressive power relies on compositional devices that set forth the sounds of nature—storms, the rustle of a brook, birds, and, of course, allusions to walking (made through the subtle loping of rhythmic figurations)—as music's very own.

Schubert owes a debt to both Mozart and Haydn, whose music he loved and whose symphonic and sacred music inspired him. Brian Newbould, a leading Schubert scholar, discerns blatant similarities of thematic construction between this symphony and Haydn's *Creation*. He also intuits several significant parallels with Mozart's popular Symphony No. 40 in G Minor, which Schubert knew well and admired. Indeed, the intervallic construction and tonal ambiance of the Adagio of the "Tragic" Symphony bears comparison, as Newbould points out, with the opening hush of Haydn's "Chaos" prelude in the *Creation*. And the jagged rush of octave unisons, as well as the instrumentation, most notably the distribution of the parts among the woodwinds, is a telling link with the finale of Mozart's Fortieth Symphony.

But all that aside, what we are left with is a work of Schubert's own remarkable invention, a succinct masterwork from the hands of a nineteen-year-old boy that even today assumes its rightful place within the pantheon of symphonic masterpieces. Its scoring was not especially innovative (it is populated by strings, winds, and timpani) and was typical of the Viennese and German chamber orchestras of Schubert's day. But its overall ambience is more optimistic than tragic, despite the somber Adagio that introduces the first movement. It was not until 1849, some twenty-one years after Schubert's death, that the Fourth Symphony was given its premiere at Leipzig, on November 19, 1849, under the baton of August Ferdinand Riccius. Its American premiere was delayed until 1935, when the New York Philharmonic performed it at Carnegie Hall.

First movement: Adagio molto—Allegro vivace

A lone pitch, C-natural, played by the full orchestra, inaugurates the beginning of the "Tragic" Symphony. For Schubert, pitch prolongation, even in this early work, had become more than a compositional *device*—a word that has no place in his musical vocabulary as it smacks of pejorative artifice and mediocrity—but took on the aura of an aesthetic strategy. Indeed, it's no accident that in his Impromptu, Op. 90, No. 1, and even at the outset of the finale of the great B-flat Major Piano Sonata, he manipulated a single pitch in much the same way, investing it with expectation. As the C-natural diminishes from *fortissimo* to a *pianissimo*, a solemn processional theme emerges, given over to the first violins and defined by a rising minor sixth that suspends its upper postulate over the bar line, only to be followed on its heels by a descending minor third (spelled here as an augmented second, from A-flat to F-sharp). As this thematic fragment dovetails surreptitiously in a chromatic ascent to a neighboring note, a pulsation of eighths whispers below in the cellos and violas. The theme is then tossed to the oboes and flutes, astride a descending, even ornamental figure played by the clarinets in a string of rapid triplets and defined by a leap of a sixth.

Though the symphony begins in C minor, Schubert's unique grasp of modulation is already at work; the Adagio's principal theme meanders quickly into wholly foreign tonal territory, surfacing barely ten bars later in G-flat major, that is, at the distance of a tritone. The tritone is one of the more peculiar elements in the musical universe; its properties are unique, in that it embodies a kind of musical duplicity. Defined as an augmented fourth, it is an interval that spans some four and a half-notes (for example, from C-natural to F-sharp) that can resolve either outward to a major sixth or inward to a major third. Moreover, the tritone is the one and only interval that implicitly embraces symmetry as it crowning achievement: no matter how you arrange it, inverting it so that one pitch stands atop or below the other, the actual interval-lic proportions remain the same. In other words, the acoustic space that separates one pitch from another never varies. Whereas a major third, for example—let's say, from C to E-natural—becomes a minor sixth when turned upside down (inverted), that is, from E to C, thus spanning six notes, the tritone minds its own business. It is a kind of intervallic chameleon capable of maintaining its intervallic shape while changing its color. The net compositional effect of such an unusual modulation, which only juxtaposes two keys at the distance of a tritone (rather than illuminating a specific interval or chord in which that interval is at play) may be lost on the average listener, save for the obvious, which is likewise set forth in the case of this Adagio. At the moment of key change, there is a palpable surprise, as if a veil had just been lifted or the sun had just burst out from behind a large gray cloud.

No sooner does Schubert alight on this G-flat major triad, pausing in cadence, then he draws us back, with nimble adjudication, to the original theme, which is restored to its tonic, C minor. Even here, the strings prevail; the woodwinds' function is perhaps more decorative than anything else, providing support as they echo the intentions and ideas of their instrumental brethren.

Enter the Allegro vivace, the principal theme of which is already recognizable as a variant of the Adagio's woeful first entry. But here the ascent of a minor sixth, from G to E-flat, is modified by the pitch material that embodies it; it is distinguished by a jumpy upbeat to its point of rest on a half-note, which occurs on the weak second beat in the ensuing bar. That this theme bears a striking resemblance to the opening of Mozart's G Minor Symphony is by no means an act of plagiarism; rather, it is an homage to a work that Schubert knew and loved, and if it is indeed a deliberately configured variant of Mozart's famous tune, Schubert makes of it a wholly individual statement.

Not only does the tempo change as the Allegro commences, but the metrical organization alters, as well; the marchlike countenance of the Adagio in 3/4 time moves into alla breve, which is essentially two beats per bar. This jaunty, rather serious theme is a nervous twitch, a staccato procession in eighth-notes introduced by the first violins against a haze of rapid repeated notes in the strings. As tension mounts in rising four-bar sequences, the theme is again given over to the first violins, whose role in the instrumental texture will dominate the entire symphony.

With the theme expanding, Schubert heightens the tension once again as it strains forward in breathless two-bar units. These are characterized by pulsating syncopes articulated by the lower strings astride abbreviated decrescendos and brusque sforzando punctuations. The hunt, so to speak, is on. A lean but lyrical second theme emerges soon enough, proceeding largely in adjacent quarter-note motion but pushing off from a lengthy half-note on the weak second beat. It, too, proceeds in sequential units, deftly modified by appoggiaturas as a means of increasing intensity. What's more, Schubert casts this second theme in A-flat major, thus challenging the usual move, in classical sonata form, to the relative major, which in this case would have been E-flat major. It's a subtle effect. Indeed, these components of its motivic design are no accident, but an emblem of organic unity, which here serves to proffer a motivic link to the Allegro vivace's principal melody. Here, Schubert adumbrates the mature music of his later years, eschewing radical contrasts of melodic design in favor of a cyclical approach that references the motivic material and key relationships of earlier movements. Likewise, he anticipates the often surprising modulations of his later music. Such compositional strategies would eventually become a hallmark of his compositional vocabulary. It appears that the teenage Schubert is still experimenting and does not dismiss the status quo but dares to challenge its traditions.

As this second subject is passed to the flutes, which echo it quietly from above, the bassoons, along with the violas and cellos, take up the slack, simultaneously inverting the tune's melodic contour. But the always adventurous Schubert, not satisfied to stay put in a single or relative key, sallies forth through E major before concluding the exposition in A-flat major, thus perpetuating an oddly quizzical relationship to the tonic key of C minor. Informing the close of this jolly exposition is a vigorous, somewhat interrogative seven-note ascending figure in eighths, born of the three-note upbeat that opened the Allegro. Now transformed and rendered autonomous, the figure alternates blithely between upper and lower registers of the strings; elsewhere, and at the same time, the woodwinds above pipe out a polonaise-type figure: two eighth-notes followed in sequence by a lightly accented quarter.

The development is nothing if not conventional for a classical sonata form, elaborating as it does the exposition's principal themes. Schubert first frames the reintroduction of that theme, now cast in B-flat minor, with a rally of ascending octave unisons that press forward and alight, in each bar, on an elongated and sharply accented second beat. The bulk of the melodic filigree here is given over to first violins, cellos, and bassoon, which press forward with the nervous principal theme as if in competition. Another handy compositional device, imitation, pits the cellos, which take up theme, against the first violins and the bassoons, which scurry for supremacy for a few anxious measures. As the texture thins out and the woodwinds take a brief hiatus, the first violins restate the theme in G minor against the thinnest stream of reiterated eighth-notes.

Here the recapitulation rears its head, albeit abruptly and as if by stealth; if there is any defiance of convention, it is the wholesale lack of preparation for the reemergence of the exposition's materials. Schubert avails himself of none of the customary techniques. There is neither a cadence nor a dramatic pause afoot, nor even so much as dominant preparation. Rather, the febrile and energetic units, of alternating eighths and quarter-notes in the aforementioned polonaise-like rhythm, simply descend and debouche without warning into the sparse restatement of the principal. But rather than revisiting it in the tonic C minor, Schubert opts for the dominant, setting it forth in the G minor. If that is not homage enough to Mozart's Fortieth Symphony, given the similarity of motivic material (the derivation of which becomes even more obvious when it is isolated by the first violins), then nothing is.

The second theme resurfaces in E-flat major, thus maintaining the identical key relationship—a distance of a minor sixth from the prevailing key of the preceding theme—that it set forth in the exposition. As the second theme, now borne aloft by the woodwinds, dissolves into the theme's consequent (a quarter-note followed first by an accentuated half-note on the second beat, and then the lightly ornamented quarter in the ensuing bar), the violins, aflutter in arpeggios, meander briefly through yet another remote key, E major. Only eight bars later, Schubert leads us back, not to the tonic C minor, but to C major.

The trumpets blare out intermittently in lengthy half-note sforzandos, and while they did the same in the exposition, here their presence yields brighter results, perhaps in deference to the major tonality to which they now pay tribute. The coda is relatively brief, taking up only eighteen bars. The strings play a sequence of ascending C major scales, which trade places with a no-less-forceful G major scale played in upward unisons by the woodwinds. With this, Schubert brings the Allegro vivace to its bright and optimistic conclusion in a resounding and life-affirming C major. So much, then, for tragedy!

Second movement: Andante

A-flat major, which informs the serenity of this stately Andante, is again Schubert's key of choice. The principal theme is carried forth by the violins against a thin accompaniment of lower strings, but for all its gentility and restraint, the theme bears at least one hallmark of romanticism: its length. The theme's mood is agile as it presses forth in 2/4 time, extending to some eight bars. A single oboe, which reiterates the fundamental motivic design that informs the principal theme, punctuates its repetition. The theme is relatively close-quartered and proceeds

in stepwise motion, and its ambience is that of consolation and acceptance. The inclusion of a raised fourth degree of the scale (D-natural)
in the sixth bar of the initial phrase is evocative enough—a forecast,
perhaps, of the unsettling events that follow in the B section.

In the wake of its lovely song, the flutes emerge with the theme and
prevail, supported in unison by the clarinets and bassoons. This they
do in alternation with the violins, which echo it. Meanwhile, the cellos
pulsate meekly on a dominant pedal point on E-flat, thus intensifying
the otherwise easy, bucolic charms of the melody. Leaving their pedal-
point post, the cellos, in sync with the dark-hued violas, take up the
motivic fragment from which the theme is fashioned and, in so doing,
lend a certain gravitas to the texture. Indeed, as the music drifts toward
the B section, and the reassuring tonic cadence that precedes it, the
music has subtly exfoliated.

The urgency of the contrasting B section forms a curious hybrid of
sorts, in that it appropriates, as the measure of its material, an ascending figure motivically akin to the spirited upbeat that inaugurated the
principal subject of the Allegro vivace. Here, Schubert shifts the compositional landscape to F minor, a key that Schubert associates with
emotional distress, consternation, and ominous prevarication. While
the violas and second violins pulsate insistently on an A-flat pedal, the
first violins, followed by the cellos, move briskly upward in a scale and
diminished arpeggio reminiscent of the opening motive of the finale of
Mozart's Piano Concerto in D Minor, K. 466. (Brian Newbould rightly
observes that the finale of Mozart's Symphony No. 39 (the "Prague")
is a likely source for this theme; no doubt it was, but the remarkable
similarity to the last movement of the Piano Concerto in D Minor is
no less coincidental.)

A delicate dialogue between the woodwinds and first violins ensues,
elaborating a middle-accented sighing motive in an array of sequential
major seconds. Only moments later, the flutes and clarinets, now in
tandem, assume responsibility for this affective sighing motive. But
here the violins take on a new shape, a nonstop sequence of repeated
sixteenths that essentially distinguish themselves as a variant of this
motive. (For those familiar with Mussorgsky's *Boris Godunov*, a nearly
identical motive is used throughout that magnificent opera to symbolize

the passage of time.) It is certainly a restless motive, one that Schubert pursues and repeats over no fewer than thirty consecutive bars. The flutes take hold of it in the last four of those thirty measures, as the oboes recapture, with soulful confidence, the principal subject.

Here the violins impose themselves yet again, bringing with them the return of the A section, not in a new key, but in the tonic A-flat major. This time Schubert fails, deliberately, to confuse or even deny our expectations. That he casts the opening theme in its home key carries with it the seeds of reassurance. The cellos and oboes complement each other yet again with their own representation of the theme's motivic fundament, only to give way to the endearing strains of the violins once more before a repeat of the B section. But now Schubert denies this newly engaged B section the advantage of its original key; here he confines it to B-flat minor, thus destabilizing our reception of its harmonic ambience and the movement's otherwise traditional harmonic trajectory. Indeed, the imposition of the raised leading tone (A-natural, just a half-tone distant from A-flat) is particularly jarring. This now-familiar, quiescent discourse, gently chided by the woodwinds against the pulsating variant of the sighing motive, diminishes in volume from a vibrant *forte* to a whispery *pianissimo* as the oboe and bassoons playfully take over the figure. But now the orchestral texture thickens slightly as a flute and clarinets engage in gentle counterpoint, quietly imposing a sequence of slurred duplets, which commence on the weak beat in the middle of each bar.

A vague recall of the ascending scale passagework that drove the Allegro vivace to its stirring conclusion is introduced by the violins for just a moment in this Andante's modest coda. Given Schubert's fondness of—and even propensity for using—such recalls as a cyclical device and psychological signpost that lends unity to structure and mood (though admittedly, in this cheerful and straightforward symphony, such links are still largely intuitive), its inclusion is likely no accident. That he gives the scale special emphasis, enlarging its dynamics to *fortissimo* at the foot of a sudden crescendo, speaks all the more convincingly for his intentions. The woodwinds, led by the flutes and clarinets, lean warmly on the principal subject en route to the coda; here, the violins and violas pulsate in *pianissimo* in a stream of repeated triplets amid the flutes and clarinets, which buttress the principal motive with docile devotion. The Andante fades to a reverent close in the distant realm of the quietest *pianississimo*.

Third movement: Menuetto—Allegretto vivace

This odd, even puckish movement, which Schubert officially designated a menuet, is for all intents and purposes a scherzo. Its mood is robust, humorous, and even a bit defiant, while its thinly painted harmonic patina is characterized by sequences of chromatic duplets that stress the upbeats and then the downbeats in every other bar. Perhaps, in calling it a menuet, Schubert merely hoped to avoid comparisons with Beethoven. Or perhaps he was just not comfortable yet in moving away from the exigencies of conventional sonata form, preferring instead to pay homage to the rococo roots of Haydn and Mozart.

Whatever the case, Schubert took pains to avoid C minor, setting the work in E-flat major, an odd choice for a rustic scherzo. The woodwinds and strings introduce the work in a jovial four-bar figure played in unison, before heightening its presence an octave higher for its first restatement. Even so, even here Schubert upsets the natural balance of the prevailing key, offering a lowered sixth (C-flat), a raised second (F-sharp), and even a raised fifth (B-natural). To be sure, B-natural is a mischievous suggestion of the very key he rejected, C minor. (B-natural is the leading tone—that is, the seventh degree of the scale that abuts the tonic—in C minor.) Within this haze of nonharmonic tones, the harmonic scheme comes under friendly fire, a kind of satirical assault that is sanctified by its victim, E-flat major. The second phase of this jaunty movement elaborates the theme in a moderately paced dialogue between strings and woodwinds.

Schubert does not abandon the convention of a trio, which forms the work's B section. The prevailing theme here, introduced by a lightly slurred, ascending upbeat over three eighth-notes, is likewise drawn from the slurred figure that anointed the movement's beginning. But here the tempo relaxes, and the slur falls over ascending intervals of a major and then a minor third. These are configured, on the first and second bars of its own four-bar phrase, as a half-note and a quarter-note.

It is a pleasant dance tune that, though relatively uneventful, is again made an object of Schubert's harmonic ingenuity. Again, he plays blithely with both the lowered sixth and third degrees of the scale (C-flat and G-flat), which become points of harmonic interest. The second phrase period, now elongated in six-bar phrases, then climbs upward, first to an E-flat and then to a C-natural. Under the baton of a savvy conductor, the reprise of the A section becomes, or ought to become, more than mere rote repetition and instead evolve into an enriched and more robust presentation of the original material.

Fourth movement: Allegro

This spirited, string-driven finale, despite a return to the principal key of C minor, sports nothing of a tragic ethos. The pace is swift, as here Schubert brings the indicated tempo, Allegro, into conformity with alla breve, a metrical designation that refers to four beats per bar divvied up into two distinct pulsations. Preceding the uneasy principal theme is a tense four-bar introduction that frames it in a sweeping C minor arpeggio colored by an F-sharp, the raised fourth degree of the C minor scale. Like the preceding movement, the inclusion of this foreign pitch (at a distance of the aforementioned augmented fourth) lends certain prescience to the proceedings, as if to give voice to a nifty Agatha Christie whodunit.

In this Allegro the woodwinds, which chirp in regularly and at intervals in imitation of the fragmented themes proffered by the violins, serve to color the texture rather than assuming any structural significance. The principal subject, carried by the violins, is a nervous affair that flies upward in two four-bar sequences, the second of which is set a whole step higher than the first. The consequent of the melody, which Schubert likewise confines to four-bar sequences, reaches its apex on the dominant pitch, G, and reproducing the rhythmic identity of the principal theme, then moves downward. Availing itself of the opening theme, a dialogue ensues among the violins, the oboes and flutes, and the bassoons and clarinets. Suddenly, the first and second violins march in, giving way to a stirring transitional passage that, in a rough-and-tumble parade of eighth-notes, extols the virtues of what had once been, some forty years earlier, the moody, nature-imitative aesthetics of Sturm und Drang. The briefest roar of the timpani, as well as a bright blare of trumpets (which Schubert uses only sparingly throughout this movement), complements the first bar of this transition, giving the listener pause to imagine, perhaps, the sonic fury of summer thunder. This flurry of notes is distinguished by their busy articulation, as each measure is organized into four pairs of alternately slurred and then staccato duplets before emerging *fortissimo* in two stormy bars of a diminished chord. The woodwinds and lower strings, confined to a pulsating accompaniment in quarter-notes, contribute to the passage's overall breathlessness.

The second theme of the exposition emerges almost imperceptibly and comprises only two notes, which Schubert sets forth as a truncated trochaic figure in the form of a descending major third. This is broadcast first by the violins and then immediately recalled, in a jovial repartee, by the clarinets, which then expand it slightly with a chromatic quarter-note ascent. The friendly competition between them does nothing to either compromise or slow down the river of eighth-notes that continue to pulsate in perpetuity—and thus in the interest of preserving rhythmic tension.

And where are the cellos in all of this? For their part, Schubert has seen fit to assign them the shallowest role, though hardly an unimportant one. As metrical mediators; they pipe out two notes per bar, on the strong first and third beats, thus providing a perky obbligato. But then, as the entire orchestra passes back and forth among its members this two-note fragment and its chromatic quarter-note anterior, the lower strings engage in a rising sequence of repeated notes. Concluding the exposition is a bold new theme in A-flat major, the first two bars of which reiterate the identical rhythm of the opening, only to be followed by a vigorous descending scale. It is no coincidence that its rhythmic design echoes, though not verbatim, the first bars of the Menuetto's happy-go-lucky trio.

A quiescent but measured trill, played by the strings, inaugurates the development and plays tag with the flutes and oboes, which carry the principal theme. A brief rest disavows the woodwinds of their preoccupation with the theme en route to a bright new tonality, in which the theme, once again extended with a playful dotted-note tag, reconfigures itself in A major. But the novelty, tension, and elaboration of these thematic fragments depend largely on key centers that migrate with increasing rapidity, and in sequences, dissolving from A major, to F major, and then to D-flat major. The rapid harmonic rhythm—that is, the rate at which one harmonic zone evaporates into the onset of another—is not so much unsettling or harmonically confrontational as buoyant. But it is also an emblem of restlessness; it foreshadows a compositional strategy, which, in so much of Schubert's later music, would become a symbol of intense longing and anxiety.

The strings again predominate the transition to the recapitulation, though here the violas and cellos command the principal theme, astride which the violins pulsate with repeated note syncopes. Elsewhere, the flutes sing out from on high, proclaiming from a stratospheric register their validity and preeminence of the slurred two-note motive of the exposition, though now it is elongated over two entire bars in whole-notes. At the same time, the secondary flutes, along with the clarinets, recycle a variant of the lyrical quarter-note tag in the corresponding place in the exposition.

The ensuing cadence on the dominant comes as rather a shock, but for reasons wholly different than it would in the composition of any other classical composer. This may be a matter of both of time and retrospect, as we have enjoyed Schubert's music for more than two hundred years. So often, in his mature music, Schubert deliberately avoids dominant preparation—that is, the introduction of the dominant key (which is based on the fifth degree of the scale and forms the strongest secondary key relationship to the home key or tonic)—en route back to the recapitulation, or as a means to frame a return to the tonic. Indeed, in the most enigmatic, bewitching, and original moments of his mature piano and chamber works, to speak nothing of his great song cycles, dominant preparation is no longer de rigueur, as it is in the classical mainstream, but expressively limited. Schubert's preferred methodology embraces frequent, often unexpected, and perpetual modulations that leave even the savviest ears unprepared for what comes next. Thus, even in this early work, in which the still-maturing Schubert embraces such rapid harmonic rhythms and innovative modulations, the appropriation of a strong dominant in such a traditional way is in itself shocking.

The four-bar introduction resurfaces, but this time in C major, and sets forth the recapitulation. Here, Schubert recasts the principal theme, too, in C major. Not satisfied with its newly clean-cut major authority, the theme migrates soon enough into A minor. Every bit of the thematic material of the exposition asserts itself again, though the reprise of the final theme in scales is perhaps enhanced by a more vigorous presence of the trumpets, now belting out their repeated notes in a militaristic polonaise rhythm. The coda hands over the thematic reins to the first and second violins, while the woodwinds and brass blurt out their long notes to thrilling effect. As if to offer a consolation prize, Schubert entrusts the principal theme, only ten bars from the end, to the woodwinds, accompanied by the strings, which interrupt with a profusion of C major chords *forte* by the strings on the weak beats. Finally, the tonic pitch, C-natural, is handed over en masse to the entire orchestra, which repeats it three times and draws the symphony to its decidedly optimistic—and most certainly not tragic—conclusion.

Symphony No. 5 in B-flat Major, D. 485

Violins 1 and 2, violas, cellos, 1 flute, 2 oboes, 2 bassoons, 2 horns in B-flat and E-flat

First movement: Allegro
Second movement: Andante con moto
Third movement: Menuetto—Allegro molto
Fourth movement: Allegro vivace

Composed only five months after his Fourth Symphony, this one, his Fifth, belies what listeners at that time, or even our own, might have expected. Though only nineteen, Schubert could already claim to be an experienced professional; indeed, that he could claim the creation of five finely crafted symphonies before he was twenty was a remarkable achievement. In his Fifth Symphony, Schubert again pays due homage to Mozart's Symphony No. 40 in G Minor, but to demean his efforts as merely derivative is as misinformed as it is inaccurate. Indeed, what he consciously or unconsciously borrowed from those masters' motivic, melodic, and harmonic vocabulary he turned into something uniquely his own. As a composer, Schubert was, from the earliest age, entirely his own man and never a lackey.

Along with his father, Franz Theodor, a violinist and cellist, and his violinist brothers, Ignaz and Ferdinand Schubert, who played the violin and viola, participated twice every week in chamber music readings. These impromptu musicales eventually drew the attention of other local musicians in Vienna, who were eager to improve their skills and gain ensemble experience. Eventually, the Schubert family's string quartet evolved into a chamber orchestra, as other musicians, including wind players, rallied to their musical cause.

This ensemble inspired and largely determined the construction of this symphony, which, given its reduced instrumental scale, makes of it something on the order of a chamber work, or more accurately, a chamber symphony. Unlike the ambitious Fourth Symphony, Schubert abandons the clarinets, timpani, and trumpets, thus reducing the work, and the listener's experience of it, to something considerably more intimate. To say that Schubert's breezy Fifth is the polar opposite of Beethoven's stentorian Fifth would be an understatement; but this complete dissimilarity also serves as evidence that Schubert, who certainly knew Beethoven's Fifth Symphony, had no interest at all in simply duplicating the centerpiece of his idol's oeuvre, much as he admired him.

Unlike Beethoven's, Schubert's status, for most of his life, was that of a working musician. He was neither celebrated nor widely published, though, as we have seen, he eventually caught the attention of several major publishers. Consequently, opportunities for the performance of his symphonic works were essentially nonexistent. His orchestral music, then, was unknown, by orchestras, conductors, and the public, which did not get wind of it until decades after his death.

Of course, today it strikes us as outrageous that one of the greatest composers of the last five centuries should never have heard his own symphonies performed, the few private and amateur readings of his earliest efforts notwithstanding. But he was at least fortunate to have heard a single performance of his Fifth, thanks to his father, who assembled a small orchestra specifically for the purpose.

First movement: Allegro

The absence of a slow, stately, and perhaps ominous introduction distinguishes this symphony from the four that preceded it. Clearly, Schubert's model for the first theme of this movement is again a subsidiary theme of Mozart's Symphony No. 40 in G Minor. But comparisons ought to stop there, as what inspired him, though certainly relevant to his creative process, was hardly identical to Mozart's masterpiece.

A four-bar frame of whispering woodwinds, played *pianissimo*, inaugurates this work. These are joined in the third bar by a vivacious descent of eighth-notes, which lead into the principal theme. Schubert divvies up the phrase periods of the next fourteen bars in an unusual manner; the fragmentary character of the principal theme, though it is succinctly presented in the first five bars following the opening frame, is elongated and elaborated. This he does by means of a lyrical descending scale that serves to connect these jolly rhythmic fragments one to the other.

The addition and elaboration of this material in the first bars of the movement has the net effect of swelling the phrase length considerably. This spreading out of the thematic material into a megaphrase, or, if you will, a long line, keeps the faith with the practices of the romantic era, which had yet to evolve. Here, it is an indication of Schubert's unique aesthetic voice coming into its own for the first time. If such a strategy seems at odds with the conventions of classical sonata form, it is not. Like any skillful composer, Schubert was hardly one to interpret these elements with rigid dispassion but instead reinvented them in a broader dynamic context. In many, even most, ways, Schubert embraced tradition, but he never allowed himself to be boxed in by it, as if a four-bar phrase period were the be all and end all of compositional technique. Certainly, if one prefers to settle for semantics over experience, then it is entirely appropriate to say that what renders the Fifth Symphony a classical work is its essentially traditional construction: around triadic formations, rather conventional key relationships, and the exigencies of sonata form.

The first violins waste no time proffering the boisterous optimism of the opening tune, a crystalline pronouncement that avails itself of an ascending B-flat major triad. This is no ordinary event, but an irresistible motivic surge that spreads out over an entire bar, only to alight thereafter on three successive F-naturals. This defining figure is repeated immediately and sequentially, first on the dominant F-major triad, and then in the subdominant E-flat. Purring away underneath are the second violins and violas, which harmonize the melody in a steady pulsation of repeated eighth-notes. Meanwhile, the cellos, in imitation of the violins, also assume the melody, tossing it between themselves and their sister violins in a fanciful dialogue. Though meagerly scored, the texture is no less robust for the exclusion of timpani, brass, and the always-endearing clarinets. What instrumental colors it may lack are more than made up for by the sheer vigor and rhythmic drive that moves this work along with such transparency. As the violins continue to make capital of the principal theme, the flutes sing out the abbreviated consequent, that is, the descending scale passage that just moments earlier fleshed out the principal thematic material. The oboes and bassoons, meanwhile, enrich the texture in a *pianissimo* halo of major and minor thirds, perfect fourths, and open fifths.

In a bold, forceful transition to the second theme, the strings and woodwinds, availing themselves of the opening subject's rhythmic (and in part motivic) formation, press forward with an alternately ascending scale, which gains momentum in a dotted rhythm and from two sforzando accents placed adroitly on the first and third beats of the bars that comprise it. A brief silence, only two beats long, precedes the entry of the lyrical second theme, which is a vague reminiscent of the principal melody, though inverted. On its heels, and with a brisk upbeat flourish, the flutes, oboes, and bassoons take over, exchanging melodic duties with the violins, which refuse to let go of a lightly ornamented fragment of the theme.

Tensions mount as a rising chromatic surge of quarter-notes, played *fortissimo* by all, morphs into a quiet reissue of the principal theme's consequent. This invigorated figure is first given over to the violins and then to the woodwinds, culminating in an imperious, arpeggiated diminished chord that brings the exposition to a close on the dominant, F major. A recall of the introductory four bars, in which the violins set forth a scale in swift descent, now serves to frame as well as inform the development. This it does, astride fragments of the principal melody, played by the flutes and oboes, for a full seventeen bars. Meanwhile, the diaphanous harmonization, which in the symphony's opening few bars, found their domicile among the woodwinds, is here transposed to the second violins, violas, and cellos. For the remainder of this relatively brief development, Schubert keeps the strings particularly busy, engaging them for several bars with an insistent motoric figure in a string of eighth-note couplets, which bump into longer quarter-note values under a slur. The cellos and violas, doubled by the bassoons, assume this responsibility, while the flutes and oboes, in cooperation with the entire violin section, reissue the thematic impulses of the exposition's elegant second theme. As the hustle and bustle of the competing instruments draws down to a hushed *pianissimo*, the flutes and oboes once again take the lead, albeit briefly, in a somewhat watered-down restatement of that same theme.

The recapitulation begins abruptly and without fanfare. Its restatement of the principal theme, in the subdominant key of E-flat major, is here subdued thanks to its unison presentation by the violins. Restating the principal material of the exposition, in respect of its classical origins, the music flies along with mercurial panache. With the return of the second subject, Schubert restores things to the home key of B-flat major. A brilliant coda played in *forte* and in unison by the full complement of strings and woodwinds (save for the horns) is nothing more than an inversion of the descending-scale passage of the work's introductory bars. The concluding measures celebrate the militaristic eighth-note salvo, which came to prominence in the development. The flutes, harmonized by the other woodwinds, taking heed, breathe their highest notes with gusto as the violins return with unimpeded vigor astride a diminished chord. The lowered sixth (G-flat) in that chord not only serves to exacerbate musical tension at the movement's eleventh hour, but also upsets our aural expectations of just how things will turn out. But come to an end they do, with the characteristic certainty that informs the overall economy of this powerful Allegro.

Second movement: Andante con moto

This lyrical confection, which by now has become an instantly recognizable tune in the household of classical music, has long since been enthroned as one of Schubert's most beloved and well-known compositions. Here, Schubert sets forth a stately, immensely appealing melody in four-part harmony as the violins give voice to the principal tune in 6/8 time. The cells of this remarkably simple formation comprise two minor thirds, the first in descent, and the second in ascent, followed by a descending minor sixth to D-natural. This in turn moves up by a half step to E-flat and is twice repeated, only to alight, at a distance of a major sixth, on a lengthy, lightly accented C-natural in the second bar. From here, the tune drifts downward in a leisurely flurry of thirty-second-notes, finding its home on the dominant pitch, F-natural.

The relatively low registration in which Schubert creates this principal tune contributes substantially to both its melodic glow and its discreet demeanor, which conveys, at least to subjective ears, an unspoken warmth and affective intensity. Indeed, this is a melody that Schubert could easily have set poetry to and invented instead as a song. The figure is reinstated, but now enriched with the participation of the woodwinds. But on this, its first repetition, it is also transposed downward by a whole step. This serves to flesh out the four-bar phrase to which it belongs and to emphasize the pristine symmetry that informs the movement's construction. Where the strings predominate in the first half of its eight-bar paragraph, the woodwinds, led by the flutes, prevail in the second.

But this efflorescent effusion, eager to continue its journey, finds itself enveloped for the next fifteen bars, by the flutes, oboes, and first violins. These deliver it in unison against the suave accompaniment of the lower strings and the dulcet octave protrusions of the horns. Though the melody announces itself in E-flat, a number of nonharmonic tones (that is, pitch material that does not specifically belong to the prevailing tonality) preside within it. Indeed, the inclusion of the lowered seventh degree of the scale (D-flat) in the midst of it all lends to this otherwise placid music a certain ambiguity. Indeed, the harmonic coloring, which veers off into transitory regions, which evoke a minor tonality, provides a prescient reminder that behind every silver lining is a cloud.

The middle (or B) section ensues in the unusual if distant key of C-flat major; but, as always in Schubert's often surprising tonal universe, things are not always what they seem to be. Indeed, the broad ascending arpeggio carried aloft in unison by the flutes, oboes, and first violins in the first four bars of the B section is the enharmonic equivalent of a simple V/7 chord in A major. The second violins and violas pulsate with a gentle stream of sixteenth-notes in perpetual motion, while above, the first violins enter into a lyrical and thoroughly Mozartean dialogue, set forth in a languishing series of major and minor thirds played by the oboes and bassoons. That its lilting melodic design is reminiscent of the slow movement (Andante) of Mozart's Piano Concerto in A Major, K 488, may be no accident, but no matter: This music, which is no less original, remains every bit equal to Mozart's.

Distinguishing the return of the A section is a slight variant of the material, which elaborates and ornaments the theme and is again entrusted initially to the first violins before being passed on to the flutes and oboes. A fourteen-bar coda briefly evokes C-flat major before drawing this lush Andante to its consoling conclusion.

Third movement: Menuetto—Allegro molto

Mozart's influence on Schubert is nowhere more apparent—even blatant—than in this serious-minded yet charming minuet, which cites the motivic material of the minuet in Mozart's Symphony No. 40. Nor is it an accident that Schubert casts it in the same key, G minor. But again, just as he did in the Fourth, Schubert transforms the material into something wholly personal, making of the ideational content an entirely unique statement; the vigorous tempo and puckish character lend it the air of a scherzo.

The work sets off with a simple, broadly arpeggiated G-minor triad, played over four bars by the entire orchestra in unison. As it swings upward from its upbeat on the fifth degree of the scale (D) toward the identical note one octave higher, four repeated notes on the same pitch bring to mind the famous opening motive of Beethoven's own Fifth Symphony. Harmonized by the lower strings, the first violins move forward on their own with a diminished chord en route to a definitive cadence on G.

But no sooner does the theme settle down than it is repeated, only to alight again on four repeated notes, but this time in a more remote key module: here, a tenuous E-flat, the sixth degree of the G-minor scale, emerges and heightens our expectations. This is turn is followed by an extended variant of the figure, now expanded into a six-bar phrase that is deftly defined, at the onset of each bar, with a descending two-note slur entrusted to the first violins and the bassoons. The motivic complement of these slurs colors the phrase with just a hint of bumptious insistence, as if in imitation of a particularly rotund dancer putting his foot down. But here, and much in the manner of a virtually identical passage in Mozart's aforementioned minuet, this A section comes to a close with a chromatically inflected descending scale passage given over to the flutes and first violins.

In the ensuing (A′) section, the identical motivic designs thus far elaborated are again revisited. The first violins survey an arpeggiated triad, albeit this time in B-flat, that is promptly followed by a rootless seventh chord, now built upon the dominant of B-flat major. This unusual key relation—the mediant, that is, at the distance of a minor third—is by now a recognizable hallmark of Schubert's restless imagination, which so often invests significance in frequent and sometimes remote modulations. Here, the first violins carry the melody over a pulsation of open fifths in the second violins, before passing it to the cellos and, from there, to the flutes high above.

A docile trio in G major ensues. Here, the first four bars engage a triad formation inspired by the motivic material of the A section. The violins, doubled by the bassoons, sing out its relaxed and bucolic ländler. The consequent that wraps up the phrase is a diatonically inflected ascent of quarter- and eighth-notes. The first violins and bassoons maintain their preeminence in the second phase of this suavely harmonized trio and proffer an elegant, lightly ornamented variant of the trio's principal theme. A canon enriches the texture here, as the flutes periodically echo the pattern. The return of the A section, reminding us yet again of its spirited charms, brings this movement to a dignified close.

Fourth movement: Allegro vivace

The playful, lightly scored eight-bar effusion that introduces this cheerful Haydnesque finale entrusts its principal theme to the first violins astride the lower strings, which lightly harmonize it with staccato punctuations. Like a dog chasing its own tail, this neatly articulated tune in 2/4 time streams by quietly in stepwise motion as it moves upward, in the first two bars, in a friendly flurry of eighth-notes. The first pair of these is conjoined by a slur, from the dominant F to the tonic, and then back again. The lively consequent that fleshes out the phrase period dances onto an accented quarter-note downbeat in advance of the repetition of the theme, now entrusted to the flutes.

A no-less-enthusiastic sequence briefly maintains the quiescent dynamic as it elaborates the eighth-note motion en route, after a brief pause, to the reprise of the principal theme in *forte*. Now the first violins play the theme again, but an octave higher, where its compatriots, the second violins, double it.

Sforzando accents lend stress to the new motivic fragment that follows, an ascending stream of half-notes, which outline a G-flat-minor triad. Revisiting the musical iconography of the Sturm und Drang era, Schubert intensifies the material with an energetic array of string tremolandos and syncopes, as well as sequences of rapid-fire sixteenth-notes, also played by the violins and cellos. A cantabile second theme emerges on the heels of a brief silence, to wit, an elongated quarter-note rest. Though taking its rhythmic cue from the principal theme, it avails itself of a seamless legato and, in its second bar, an expressive downward leap of a minor sixth. These are supported by the second violins, which proffer the rhythmically identical eighth-note figure, now modified by a slur on the first beat of each bar. A prescient consequent in F minor is enlisted by the woodwinds but led by the flutes in descending double thirds. A carefree procession of triplets, again presided over by the violins, imposes a certain buoyancy to the musical texture, drawing the exposition to its close in F major, a conventional harmonic choice for a most unconventional composer.

The development takes advantage of the rhythmic contours of the principal theme, though now elaborating it in a chromatically inflected, fragmentary span of six ascending notes, the first five of which proceed in eighths before alighting on a quarter. Schubert sets these optimistic if mercurial fragments in a lively dialogue, passing them in succession among the strings and the woodwinds.

Commencing with a sforzando placed adroitly above a downbeat on a dominant seventh chord, ten bars of dominant preparation—a compositional procedure that Schubert would often abandon in his later compositions—lead to the recapitulation. Save for the reprise of the second theme in the tonic key of B-flat, this recapitulation is an identical rebroadcast of the exposition. Curiously, perhaps in an effort to mimic the practices of the classical-era chamber symphony, Schubert denies the movement a coda, bringing things to their dignified close just as he did in the exposition, albeit in the home key of B-flat major.

Symphony No. 8 in B Minor, D. 759 ("Unfinished")

Violins 1 and 2, violas, cellos, basses, flutes, oboes, clarinets, bassoons, horns, trumpets in pairs, 3 trombones, timpani
Composed in October 1822. Score discovered by Sir George Grove and Arthur Sullivan in 1865.
First performance by the Vienna Musikverein in December 1865, conducted by Johann Herbeck.

First movement: Allegro moderato
Second movement: Andante con moto

The manner in which fanciful sobriquets are imposed on musical compositions invites critique. Whether the imaginative fantasies of a composer's whim or a publisher's colorful moniker will benefit a work's popularity and sales remains to be seen. Certainly, the name "Unfinished," which has long been attached to Schubert's two-movement

Eighth Symphony, was not of his own making. The title is in part due to the existence of a sketch of a third movement, a scherzo, that appeared to prove his intent to flesh out the work into a conventional symphonic edifice. Additionally, scholars have speculated that Schubert intended to tack on, as this symphony's finale, the Entr'acte for the incidental music to his *Rosamunde*. Whatever the case, although the Eighth Symphony's two complete, complementary movements are each a masterpiece of form and content, the mystery of what might have been has never failed to hold a certain allure.

Indeed, it is only by proxy that the B Minor Symphony has for so long borne the number "Eighth" at all, and even to this day there is some dispute over that assignment. That is because the Seventh Symphony, in E major, was originally no more than an elaborate sketch, of which only the introduction was actually written out and fully scored.

Speculation has long prevailed in connection with the genesis and history of the Unfinished Symphony, and the reasons that Schubert left it incomplete, if he in fact did so. Some people are convinced that, for aesthetic reasons, Schubert ultimately decided that his musical agenda was best served in the form of a masterful torso, wherein the first and second movements are in entirely different keys. This perspective holds that Schubert, convinced of the import of the work's musical message, was eager that it be preserved for future generations to admire. This view would appear to gain ground given his preoccupation with other projects that engaged him simultaneously, not the least of which was the Wanderer Fantasy. Could it be that prior commitments and material concerns, especially the unlikelihood of convincing, much less underwriting a decent orchestra to perform it, convinced him that two movements would suffice?

It is only too easy to invest in another popular myth, namely, that when he composed the work in 1822 he already knew his death was imminent, having learned of the syphilis that would eventually kill him. That would presuppose a conviction on his part that the Unfinished Symphony, which he certainly knew to be a gigantic advance in his artistic development, ought be brought to public attention without delay.

A more reasonable explanation, advanced by Brian Newbould, is that the work was indeed meant for elaboration, and that the existence of the scherzo sketch is proof enough. Furthermore, Newbould observes, Schubert probably did not contract syphilis until 1823, after the Unfinished was, well, finished. What is true is that in 1823, Schubert entrusted the score to his friend Huttenbrenner, whom he charged with making of it a gift to the Styrian Music Society in Graz, which had recently awarded him official membership in its prestigious organization. For that Schubert, who had not achieved anything even remotely close to Beethoven's celebrity, was grateful. But to presume that even this otherwise august honor moved him to submit the symphony in an abbreviated state with no intention of completing it at a later date says less about his judgment than it does about his intentions. Like any composer worth his salt, especially in the light of the potentially important opportunity the Styrian Society afforded, Schubert would likely have preferred to contribute something that represented his compositional powers at their peak. Certainly, the two completed movements of the symphony did just that, but it is difficult to imagine that Schubert, eager to take advantage of the opportunity, did not expect a relationship with the society that would eventually allow him to express himself in whatever way he saw fit.

But the notion that he merely abandoned any interest in fleshing out the Eighth seems unreasonable. Nor is this idea supported by the facts. It was hardly uncommon at the time for a composer to deliver an unfinished work with a promise to complete it at a later time, and as Newbould rightly points out, the performance of single movements of a composition was at that time customary. That he also held on to his piano sketches, including the scherzo, until his death, suggests that Schubert might well have conceived of a larger entity worthy of revisiting.

Whatever the case, the Unfinished Symphony languished in obscurity for some forty-two years before Johann Herbeck, the conductor of the Musikverein Orchestra, persuaded Huttenbrenner to entrust the score to his care for its premiere performance on December 17, 1865. Though reluctant to do so, Huttenbrenner could not have been unhappy that Edwin Hanslick, a critic whose wide influence and stature endeared him to Brahms, took note of the reaction of the Viennese public to what until then had been a long-lost masterpiece. "When, after the introductory bars, the oboe and clarinet give out their suave melody in unison over the quiet murmur of the violins, any child could have recognized the authorship; and a stifled exclamation, almost a whisper, ran through the hall: Schubert!"

First movement: Allegro moderato (CD Track I)

The absence of an extended introduction in the opening eight bars of this Allegro moderato is significant, and it forms the source of its mysterious atmosphere. Indeed, the lean orchestration that entrusts the introductory theme, which is neither identical to nor formally configured as the principal subject, to a quiet hush of cellos and basses embraces ambiguity from the very first note. As played in union by these brethren of strings, the mood it sets is somber. Schubert holds his melodic intent close to his vest. Set in the customary 3/4 time signature of a waltz, the murky underpinnings of the opening salvo commence with the tonic pitch, B-natural, en route, in an ascending scale, to D-natural only one bar further. But then, as if unwilling to aspire to brighter harmonic pastures, the second half of the theme descends in disjunct motion to a D-natural an octave below, before settling, for three entire bars, on the dominant F-sharp.

With that, Schubert established one of the most recognized melodies in the history of Western art music, though perhaps not so famous as the lyrical second subject that follows it some minutes later. But first, the movement's principal melody assumes its stature in Schubert's symphonic diaspora. That Schubert delays its entrance for four bars, separating it from the introductory material with a nervous, melodically contoured figure in the lower register of the violins, is significant. Indeed, within its confines Schubert has raised the compositional stakes, as it were, in making its steady stream of sixteenth-notes something far greater than mere accompaniment. The figure itself accedes to the status of a melody, though its function as such is supported entirely by its harmonic profile, which surveys the B-minor scale in its natural and melodic forms (alternating the sixth-degree G-natural with G-sharp) as a means of heightening tension.

As this busy but quiescent figuration thrives below, continuing to percolate for twenty-seven bars atop the lower strings' periodic pulsations in eighths, the oboes and clarinets pipe out their haunting charge, which now gains ground as the principal subject. Though motivically and rhythmically unremarkable, it is a sad tune. Its simplicity is assured by the prolongation, over an entire bar, of a lone F-sharp—the home pitch of the dominant—which then falls to the tonic B, before moving upward, in ascending eighth-notes, back to F-sharp. Following an immediate repetition of the subject, its consequent draws itself out over the next four bars with an ascent to a pungent F-natural. Already Schubert is up to his old tricks, manipulating our senses and aural expectations with shrewd assurance as he introduces foreign pitch material, albeit so far in related rather than unrelated tonalities. The flutes and bassoons pick up the slack in a transitory passage as the business of the first subject is concluded. With the orchestral texture thus enriched, things move forward in an inexorable ascent of stacked major and minor thirds, modified by a steady crescendo. But then, in a highly unusual move, the bassoons and horns appropriate only four bars in preparation for second subject, a theme that has by now become a household melody known even to those who may not be able to identify its composer.

The cellos set sail with this celebrated eight-bar tune, which bears only a vague rhythmic resemblance to the principal subject. It is a gentle though sweeping cantabile, whose positioning in G major contradicts the disquieting anxiety of the preceding section. Set against discreet pulsating syncopes embodied by the clarinets, violas, and, later, the bassoons, it proceeds with imperturbable assurance before being taken over by the violins, which quietly echo its song with restraint.

Following a single bar of silence, a sudden plunge into an abrasive *fortissimo*, set in motion by a sequence of string tremolos on a C-minor triad—yet another remote tonality—pushes its way upward in a vigorous arpeggio duly modified with a C-sharp and F-sharp, both constituents of the B-minor scale. To say that this harmonic potpourri, transitional though it may be, is merely tense would be an understatement; it is nothing if not terrifying—an emblem, you might say, of pure panic. Moments such as these distinguish the mature, profoundly inspired Schubert from the immensely gifted one of the Fourth and Fifth symphonies.

Dissolving into the same pattern of breathy syncopes that accompanied the second subject, the woodwinds form an advance team in preparation for the elaboration of that famous melody, now fragmented and tossed between the lower and upper strings in an increasingly animated dialogue. As these thematic fragments pile up with cumulative abandon, they are distinguished one from another by means of articulation and dynamics; the decibel level swells to *fortissimo* while their heretofore legato constituents are transformed into a martial, staccato stride. But these are interrupted with a flourish of sforzando chords that Schubert sets firmly on the weak beats of all but one of the ensuing seven bars.

On the heels of these seven bars, the second subject, self-satisfied for its loveliness, presses suavely forward in a velvety legato and is made the centerpiece of canonic imitation. No sooner do the first violins—followed imitatively by the second violins and then the cellos—recall the melody than they are pursued, in the same fashion, by the flutes, oboes, and bassoons. The woodwinds alight on a G-major triad in diminuendo, prolonging it for some five bars atop the pizzicato pronunciations of the lower stings, which give shape to a descending B-minor scale.

Where a less imaginative composer might well have made the most capital out of the enormously appealing second subject of the exposition, elaborating it ad infinitum in the development, Schubert does no such thing, choosing instead to confound our expectations. The brooding introductory theme heard at the outset of the development is once again given over darkly to the cellos and basses in unison. But only nine bars after its reintroduction in the subdominant E minor, a tense and mysterious variant, distinguished by an alteration of its thematic design, comes into play. Here the melody, carried in *pianissimo* by the first and second violins and made subject to imitation by the violas and bassoons astride an uneasy tremolo in the lower strings, angles inexorably upward to a B-natural. This resolves onto a chromatically altered chord, akin to a French sixth, the apex of which, in this instance, is an A-sharp.

For those who may be unfamiliar with the vocabulary of harmony, have no fear. Suffice it to say that chords of this variety—(augmented) sixth chords, of which there are several subspecies—imbue their harmonic surroundings with a certain instability and a sense of longing (which, in compositional terms, is a longing for resolution to a more stable, or key-centered, environment). Sixth chords have a strong tendency to resolve onto the dominant (the fifth degree of the scale within the prevailing key they modify). In compositional parlance, this function is called a secondary (or derived) dominant.

Schubert's elaboration of these chords throughout this development is visionary. Decades later, at the turn of the twentieth century, a very different kind of composer, the Russian Alexander Scriabin (1872–1915), would turn the potential of sixth chords, and their harmonic constituents, into a virtual cause célèbre and influenced compositional theory and aesthetics for generations to come.

Brian Newbould interprets this passage as being born of a Neapolitan relation, which is yet another secondary dominant, built on the second degree of the scale rather than the sixth. In this case, the harmony is related to B minor, but also to C major, given the alternating presence of a C-natural and a C-sharp within the texture. Though the recapitulation ends up in B minor, the reigning ambiguity of the passage, as Newbould rightly observes, is precisely what drives it and keeps us, as listeners, on our toes.

The eerie countenance of this uneasy harmonic reservoir is made all the more anxious with the materialization of a pungent dominant ninth a few bars later, when the first tag (E–F-sharp–G) of the theme is inverted and relentlessly repeated in unison by the violins, cellos, flutes, and oboes for twelve bars. But Schubert, unwilling to stop there or provide even a modicum of relief, presumes to heighten the tension even more, alighting *fortissimo* on a descending C-sharp-minor triad, slowly arpeggiated across five bars. But even this is rendered rhythmically ambiguous by the pulsating syncopes—a significant figure that returns in the second movement—made so familiar to us in the exposition. Oddly, this now pervasive accompaniment finds itself all alone; the docile theme that it once supported is nowhere to be found, as if it had just lost the one thing in the world it loved. In musical terms, and for the savvy listener who is aware of it, the sense of loss made conspicuous by its absence is palatable. This arpeggiated figure then dissolves into a sequence of secondary dominants, which eventually find their way back to a *fortissimo* restatement of the entire introductory theme, now broadcast in tutti and firmly entrenched in the development's home key, E minor.

What follows is a booming, *fortissimo* variant of the sixteenth-note figure, again entrusted to the violins but now configured in ascent. But here Schubert imposes the introductory tune in the cellos and bases, which are joined by the whistling treble of the woodwinds. The trumpets, trombones, and timpani lend their ominous support, as if to issue a sepulchral warning, from below.

Only nine bars into this profusion, the oboes, horns, trumpets, and timpani introduce a belligerent dotted-eighth-note figure on a single pitch. The violin violins, viola, flutes, and clarinets hold court with a rapid upbeat flourish, followed by an unforgiving, insistent reiteration of the second tag, in disjunct motion, of the introductory theme. The rapid thirty-second-note upbeat flourishes that ornamented the texture only moments earlier then return with vehemence, but now in succession. They are configured within each bar as a compound appoggiatura (that is, as several nonharmonic tones, or *leaning* notes played on, rather than ahead of, the beat). The clarinets and bassoons, murmuring a stepwise variant of the principal (but not the introductory) theme of the exposition, now set forth in a progression of double thirds, which precede a hushed, chromatically inflected oscillation in the flutes and oboes.

With this, the recapitulation emerges stealthlike, commencing with a reprise of the sixteenth-note figure, again played *pianissimo* and carried by the violins in the tonic key of B minor. The now all-too-familiar second subject, given over first to the cellos and then passed to the violins, resurfaces in D major. Given Schubert's proclivity to defy convention and migrate to far-flung tonal regions, it is perhaps surprising in a work of this maturity that he would so willingly accede to the ground rules of traditional sonata form. But maybe such conformity, in light of his harmonic ingenuity, is in itself the stuff of surprise. The round of imitation, which, in the exposition, elaborated the second subject, shines through here in like fashion. The coda is a succinct affair of some forty-one measures that reestablishes the introductory theme of the movement's opening bars.

The cellos and basses, followed by the violins, quietly revisit the first few notes of the introductory theme. But on this occasion the woodwinds and trombones expand it in a replay of the anxiety-ridden chromatic oscillation that informed the opening of the development. A mighty crescendo draws the entire orchestra forward into a *fortissimo* B-minor triad, which immediately dissolves into a dominant seventh chord. B minor, now tamed by a *pianissimo*, returns. On the back of the first three notes of the introductory motive, the clarinets and oboes issue a plaintive cry, which is then doubled by the flutes and upper strings in a hairpin crescendo and decrescendo—from *mezzo forte* to *forte* to *pianissimo*. The cellos and basses, not to be outdone, then fortify the fragment on their own terms, as the trumpets, horns, bassoons, and clarinets harmonize it in the orchestral shadows.

Second movement: Andante con moto

The ambulatory tempo that inaugurates this Andante is representative of Schubert's aesthetic sensibility, as well as that of his era. The codification of natural phenomena, established in poetry and painting, had long since become all the rage in music. People's relationship to the passage of time in the early nineteenth century was significantly different than for audiences today. Time was perceptible for its passing, as it is now, but there seemed to be more of it. The quotidian events that demarcated it and engaged early nineteenth-century perception were not ruled by technology, nor by the expectation of immediate gratification. On the contrary, the passage of time was something to be experienced naturally, at a pace commensurate with the sensibility, objectives, and resources of the era.

In the absence of instantaneous electronic communication, high-speed travel, and all the technological accoutrements we now take for granted, time was measured in quite another way. The presence and use value of art, literature, poetry, and music demanded contemplation by a populace that took them seriously.

This gracious Andante con moto, which unfolds with such euphonious assurance, evokes the sounds and sights of nature. That it does so without relying on any specific program provided by its composer (though, as Charles Fisk and others have persuasively suggested, Schubert's short story *Mein Traum*, which he wrote only months earlier, may well have served as its inspiration) is a credit to its efficacy. Nor do any specific compositional clichés (tremolandos for storms, descending staccato thirds for birdcalls, etc.) deny our individual imaginations the right to envision such matinal imagery. The music of this Andante appeals with its simple bucolic song and a harmonious patina, replete with mnemonic recalls from the first movement, that are as guileless and perfectly integrated as a country garden or a lakeside forest.

Things take shape with the bassoons and horns angling upward in fourths and sixths, and in contrary motion to a descending E-major scale in the bass. Charles Fisk shrewdly suggests that its melodic identity is not unique, but a direct citation of a motivic fragment from Schubert's lied "Der Wanderer" (The Wanderer), D. 489.The fragment accompanies the words "Ich wandle still, bin wenig froh" (I wander silently and am somewhat unhappy). The horns here not only serve a compositional purpose, informing the orchestration; they are also a constituent of landscape aesthetics. Like his contemporaries, Schubert dispatched the horn as a torchbearer for nature itself. In a nod to the strategy of the first movement, these few bars serve as an introduction to the principal theme proper, which emerges in the violins and violas only three bars later. This five-bar thematic fragment is no less sparse, surveying a stepwise ascent from B to C-sharp, followed by the lilting descent of an E-major triad that alights, in the next bar, on F-sharp. Like the breaking of the dawn, this gentle theme comes gradually into view and is framed, with each successive appearance, by the motivic material, now in contrary motion, which defined the opening.

Schubert does not fail to elaborate his inspired theme, and he colors it with a lowered sixth (C-natural) that augurs a docile arc of successive sixteenth-notes. It's an impressionistic touch, to be sure, a gentle rivulet evocative of a running stream. As he widens the registrational expanse of the orchestral texture to include the cello's doubling of the descending bass line, the flutes and oboes sing out the ascending introductory motive (and the subsequent rivulet tag) above. The aural environment, thus illumined in higher registers and by the lofty woodwinds, assumes a metaphorical ambience that suggests the breaking of the dawn. Though musical imagery of this sort is a matter of subjective interpretation, we can perceive its bucolic implications. This association may arise from our collectively conditioned and inherited musical reflexes, which deduce, however illogically, such evocative imagery from such effusive harmonies and fluid rhythms.

A new phase of the introductory fragment then comes to roost in a robust *forte*, wherein the entire string section, in unison with the trombones, carries the descending scale motive. In stark contrast to the preceding material, the musical provenance here turns aggressive, bold, and even gruff. Elsewhere, the woodwinds and trumpets hold forth with their end of the introductory material, which now rises richly in thirds and sixths. Varying the texture yet again, the flutes and clarinets assume the principal theme. The violins, eager to respond, then engage the rivulet tag, and do so from the colorful perch of a C-natural—the lowered sixth degree.

Just as he did in the exposition and recapitulation of the first movement, Schubert barely prepares the entrance of the second subject, choosing instead to introduce its accompaniment figure in advance. The first violins, standing alone, ascend by an octave to a G-sharp, before plunging onto a syncopated pulsation—a recall of a near-identical figure that accompanied the second subject in the first movement—now supported by the violas, that establishes the new key, C-sharp minor. A solo clarinet, playing *pianissimo*, carries the new subject; it is a distant, plaintive wail in a sequence of rising major and minor thirds, with a single pitch dominating each bar.

As always, Schubert finds piquant pleasure in unexpected modulations to alien keys: hints of D major mix and alternate blithely with attenuated strains of F major in the string accompaniment. The second phase of this theme likewise exploits sequence of thirds, though now with two, then three notes per bar, which intensifies the pace. Following the tune's gentle ascent to a sustained G-sharp, it is repeated, but here an oboe, sounding lonely and forlorn, has appropriated it. Below, the cellos echo a fragment of the second subject, reiterating an elongated downbeat (a dotted quarter-note) with a subtle accent. Rounding off the theme, which has now modulated into D-flat major, is a variant of the sixteenth-note rivulet tag of the opening bars, tossed back and forth between a solo oboe and a flute.

Mysteriously, the prevailing dynamic has been reduced to *pianississimo*, a unique occurrence in Schubert's orchestral music; until now he had never ventured into an acoustic space so quiescent and thus subject to the especially radical contrast with what follows. Without warning, the dynamic expands to *fortissimo*. The lower strings draw out the second subject astride a strident countersubject in rising disjunct motion played by the violins at three eighths to the bar. This booming countersubject is no mere accompaniment, but a driving force that lends weight and power to the rhythmic trajectory and harmonic scheme. It is also a liberal variant of the earlier accompaniment, likewise taken up by the strings, that elaborated the introductory theme following the first two statements of the principal subject. The staccato markings that modify it ought not be construed to mean that each note in the passage should be pinched, strangled, or otherwise robbed of its breadth. On the contrary, an articulation of this sort is an indication that each successive pitch is to be rendered separate from the other, but without compromising its resonance. Schubert is not finished yet, pulling out all the stops as the flutes double the countersubject. Elsewhere, the violins and oboes expand the descending scale motive of the movement's first two bars into a descending fury of thirty-second-notes.

The cellos and basses usher in the development, where the second subject is revisited, again preceded by a syncopated accompaniment in the second violins and violas. Moments later the first-violin section moves in, assuming the theme in a wistful, quasi-canonic dialogue with the lower strings. A flute and oboe, modified by a long diminuendo, then assume the motive in a wistful exchange with the bassoons and horns. Here the development winds down; the horns anticipate the recapitulation by giving voice to a drooping duplet, three times articulating the interval of an octave in descent as if it were a sigh of regret. The return to E major restores the exposition's principal themes, which blossom here with disarming ease as the horns restating the hush of the introductory chords.

The second subject emerges again, this time in A minor, though its coloring has been altered: an oboe has taken over the duties that had, in the exposition, been assumed by the clarinet. But no sooner do they yield the tune than the clarinet commandeers it once again. The following passage duplicates the thematic material of the exposition but reverses the roles of the strings. This time the violins sing out the second subject, while the lower strings take responsibility for the bellicose countersubject. The ensuing run of thirty-second-notes in *moto perpetuum*, now cast in E minor, gains the support of the cellos, which mimic it in unison. Only seven bars later, the basses and bassoons do the same.

A succinct coda revisits all the introductory and principal themes, commencing with an expanded variant of the introductory chords, which now ascend to a high B-natural in the flutes before coming to rest on the tonic two bars later. The orchestral texture thins, evaporating into the strains of the first violins alone, which outline an E-major triad. As the clarinets and bassoons reissue a tag of the principal subject, enriched by the bass trombones below, the tonal landscape briefly shifts to A-flat major, the enharmonic equivalent of the E major's mediant, G-sharp major. Following the violins' and cellos' lilting reiteration of the ever-so-fluid rivulet tag, the movement draws to a close much as it began: in contrary motion. The flutes and oboes carry the ascending chords of the introductory theme as the lower strings unfurl their pizzicatos in descent.

There is little sense here in discussing the extant sketch for a third movement, a scherzo in B minor, which Schubert penned only as a piano score (though he did at least begin to draft it for orchestra); even that was incomplete, as the trio section boasts only a single melodic line. Regarding the speculation that Schubert intended to tack on, as the fourth movement, the entr'acte from *Rosamunde*, he composed *Rosamunde* at a devil's pace and under pressure in 1823, most likely in less than a month, and its orchestration is virtually identical to that seen in the Unfinished. What's more, as Brian Newbould has scrupulously observed, it is an unusually massive work, in full-blown sonata form, thus contradicting its role as incidental music, which is normally abbreviated. Its key, B minor, and its motivic similarities to the scherzo fragment strengthens the notion. Whatever the case, no one knows for certain what might have dissuaded him from expanding the Eighth Symphony's two movements into four, nor does it really matter. Perhaps he was dissatisfied with it, or wanted to get on with more pressing artistic matters. We can only be thankful that the two movements that constitute the "Unfinished" Symphony as we know it today, and which add up to a cultural monument of inimitable proportions, survive at all.

Symphony No. 9 in C Major, D. 944 ("The Great")

Violins 1 and 2, violas, cellos, basses, 3 flutes, 3 oboes,
    2 clarinets, 2 bassoons, 4 French horns, 2 trumpets, 3
    trombones, tuba, timpani, percussion, harp, and strings
Completed in 1826
The first performance, in an edited version, took place in
    Leipzig on March 21, 1839, with the Leipzig Gewandhaus
    Orchestra conducted by Felix Mendelssohn. The first complete
    performance was in Frankfurt, 1841.

First movement: Andante—Allegro, ma non troppo
Second movement: Andante con moto
Third movement: Scherzo—Allegro vivace
Fourth movement: Allegro vivace

The genesis of the Ninth Symphony, at least with regard to its numeric position in the catalogues of Schubert's symphonic works, was a confusing affair for most of the nineteenth and even the twentieth century. Even to this day, though it is now widely regarded as the Ninth, it is also occasionally referred to, at least by some programmers and cataloguers, as his Seventh or Eighth. But why?

Schubert penned the work in 1825 while on holiday in Bad Gastein and Gmunden in Austria. Though he essentially completed it a year later, he couldn't resist making revisions as late as 1827. Like so much of his music, the Ninth Symphony was neither published nor performed in the composer's short lifetime, and his hopes of having it performed by the Gesellschaft der Musikfreunde in Vienna, to which he dedicated it, were soon dashed. There is some dispute as to why it was summarily rejected by that august organization, despite its having paid Schubert one hundred guilders, roughly the equivalent of $56 in today's U.S. currency.

The confusion over how to number Schubert's works has stemmed from the total lack of their categorical organization during his lifetime. Given the absence of a committed publisher who, had he aligned himself with Schubert early on in his career, would have had the presence of mind to do just that, as well as the fact that only a handful of his works (approximately a hundred out of more than a thousand completed works) were published before Schubert's death, much was left to speculation.

Adding to the confusion was Sir George Grove's discovery of the Eighth ("Unfinished") Symphony in 1867, though it was Sir George himself who eventually determined that the "Great" was, or ought to be, Schubert's Ninth. Indeed, this English editor of the most comprehensive encyclopedia of music ever compiled ultimately resolved that the extant and comprehensive sketch for the E Major Symphony should be labeled Schubert's Seventh, at least in England. That decision in turn led Sir George to insert the "Unfinished" Symphony as the Eighth of the batch. But things get stickier still, given that Schubert's own brother, Ferdinand, who took it upon himself to become the chief archivist and caretaker of the music after the composer's death, had labeled the "Great" as the Seventh!

If you think that's labyrinthine, consider this: Alois Fuchs, another Schubert archivist who labored to assemble a thematic catalogue of the music in the 1840s, blithely refers to the sketch of the E Major Symphony (today's number seven) as the Eighth Symphony. Fuchs set aside a place in his catalogue for another symphonic work, possibly Schubert's last unfinished work, which would have been his Tenth Symphony. Since neither Fuchs nor Ferdinand was even aware of the existence of the "Unfinished" at that time (remember, Schubert had discreetly entrusted the score to his friend Huttenbrenner, with a view toward making a gift of it to the Styrian Music Society in Graz), it is wholly unlikely that the blank entry in the Fuchs's catalogue had been reserved for that masterpiece. But even the noble efforts of Otto

Deutsch—the dean of all Schubert cataloguers, whose "D" numeric organization prevails for Schubert's music—were reinterpreted by his revisionists Arnold Feil and Walter Durr as recently as 1978. At that time, Feil and Durr once again recommended that the "Unfinished" be labeled the Seventh Symphony and the "Great," the Eighth Symphony.

Now that we've cleared that up, the work itself deserves better than the methodical accounting of a musical numismatist. After all, this is the work that utterly enthralled Robert Schumann, who put it on the map after persuading Ferdinand Schubert to entrust him with the manuscript. Though it took him some years to convince the musical establishment of its worth, he eventually won the day when he turned the score over to Mendelssohn, who gave the first, albeit heavily edited, performance of it in Leipzig in 1839, some eleven years after Schubert's death. In his article about the work for the *Neue Zeitschrift für Musik* on March 10, 1840, Schumann referred to the work's "heavenly length," a remark that eventually took on a celebrated life of its own and was used by scholars, annotators, and the public alike to describe, often unfairly and inaccurately, many of Schubert's other works.

While it is true that, with the repeats kept intact, the Ninth Symphony can stretch to nearly an hour, its temporal dimensions are fundamentally irrelevant to its most salient features, not the least of which are its structural economy, inspired content, and aesthetic integrity. It would be difficult to imagine even a single composer who followed in Schubert's footsteps who does not owe a debt to it, including even his most vicious critics, not the least of whom was Richard Wagner, who jealously dismissed Schubert as merely second-rate. And yet, for all that, who cannot hear, in the opening strains of *Das Rheingold*, for example, more than a hint of the harmonic invention of the Ninth's first-movement Allegro? Certainly, Schubert's influence e on Schumann was profound; it is no accident that shortly after becoming familiar with the Ninth, Schumann penned his ravishing song cycle *Dichterliebe*.

As we shall see, this, the last full-fledged orchestral work Schubert ever wrote, is all about economy. Its structural underpinnings reveal themselves within the first eight bars and become, in one guise or another, the basis for thematic and rhythmic invention throughout the entire symphony. Formally, the Ninth's sympathies lie with the conventions of the classical era, despite the somewhat asymmetrical pattern given voice by the important principal theme of the first movement's introductory Andante. That Schubert could have composed something so entirely original only a few years after the premiere of Beethoven's own Ninth is astonishing enough, though slyly refers, in the finale, to the latter's *Ode to Joy*. This reference was not, of course, anything on the order of plagiarism or even allusion, but simply a tip of the hat to the master he revered—to the one artist he could have called his equal had he only possessed the confidence to do so.

First movement: Andante—Allegro, ma non troppo

It is no secret, as we have already observed, that the absence or inclusion of an introduction, in the first movement of a symphonic work in sonata form, can assume structural significance, depending on which way the compositional winds blow. Indeed, in the classical era the introduction was usually set in a moderate to slow tempo as it bespoke the grandeur of a wizened, avuncular storyteller, as if to say "Far away, and many years ago, there lived . . . ." Schubert makes no attempt to dismiss this favored apparatus as merely old-fashioned or insufficiently inventive. Instead he chooses to embrace it, energize it, and make it his own.

Though he was born at the tail end of the classical era, Schubert lived and worked on the cusp of the nineteenth century's burgeoning romanticism. That he put his compositional resources to work in the interest of elevating a traditional form to the status of something innovative was astonishing enough, particularly in the still-warm glow of Beethoven's own Ninth Symphony, which had had its premiere only a few years earlier. While no one, including the composer himself, would ever hear Schubert's Ninth in his lifetime (save for a scanty read-through by the Musikverein that never blossomed into a performance), its larger influence on Schumann, Brahms, Bruckner, and Mahler should not be underestimated. This Andante could not have been more significant to that influence, given its compositional function in relation to the entire symphonic edifice; virtually every motivic constituent that reveals itself in the opening bars informs not only the remainder of the movement, but the entire work.

A simple but noble theme introduces the work and is broadcast by the horns. Schubert's choice to use horns to announce what amounts to the national anthem of this symphony is in itself meaningful, as their soft, if brassy, sound had long been emblematic of nature. The theme itself is remarkable for a certain lack of symmetry, and an examination of its contours may prove valuable. The germ of the theme, which is in 4/4 time, is stated succinctly in the first two bars, wherein a lightly accented half-note on the tonic, C, is followed by two breathy quarter-notes in stepwise ascent to E-natural. The second bar takes a dip to the sixth degree of the scale, A-natural, and more or less reverses the rhythmic design. It also accents a dotted quarter-note that angles up gently, again in stepwise motion, to the tonic C half-note, which is again an accented half-note. The next bar, which starts out on the subdominant (the fourth degree of the scale) F-natural, serves only to duplicate the rhythmic design of that preceding figure, albeit in reverse. This time it descends to an E-natural. As the melody leans upward in the next measure to the dominant G, the pattern of the first bar is repeated, and then the following, fifth, bar is a clone of the second bar.

Creeping upward yet again with the identical rhythm, the sixth bar gives prominence to a D-natural that drifts downward, via its neighbor E-natural, to a C-natural, thus yielding to the gravitational pull of the tonic, around which the entire phrase orbits. The next two bars, which wrap up the theme, are significant for their difference. For one thing, the downbeats in bars seven and eight remain unaccented, contradicting the pattern Schubert has thus far established, in which the first beat in every one of the first six measures has borne the brunt of emphasis, codified with an accent above the note. But there is something else, too: in these two bars, Schubert prolongs the pitch material and rhythmic design of the sixth measure, extending or "augmenting" them—which is to say, doubling the note values—while also relaxing the dynamic tension as the theme diminishes from a hushed *piano* to an even quieter *pianissimo*. Thus does the phrase divvy up into two distinct groups, like a subject and predicate; the first group comprises the first three bars, while the second comprises the remaining five, including the unusual two-bar closing tag in augmentation.

The importance of this particular melodic fragment will become apparent soon enough. As the initial theme draws to a close, the woodwinds, save for the flutes, assume the theme and, along with the strings below, harmonize it with gentle dispatch. Just then, the violins and violas yield a descending six-note tag of two quarter-notes, followed by a triplet oscillation that fades out on a quarter-note. Languishing under a slur, this contrasting figure, enriched by a suave legato, conveys a certain assurance as it fortifies the proceedings. Within moments, the viral compulsion born of the principal theme emerges as the violins change their tune, literally; all at once they step forward with a stepwise variant of the theme now modified by pizzicato.

As the woodwinds fade, the violas and cellos echo the themes' implicit design. Here the entire string section enrolls the support of the tenor and bass trombones in a *fortissimo* pronouncement of the theme that dovetails the quiet, distant, and obedient response of the woodwinds, which give voice to the theme's consequent, a reiteration of the movement's third bar. Tensions increase as the theme marches forward in unison, borne aloft by the strings and trombones in unison, while the woodwinds articulate its now already familiar rhythms, with unusual insistence, en route to the distant key of A-flat major.

The modulation is only temporary; C major is hardly ready to give up its reign. As the woodwinds, led by the oboes and absent the flutes, regurgitate the principal theme—whose presence, by the way, has by now become utterly ubiquitous—the violins, in conjunction with the steady quarter-note motion of the cellos and basses, bring forth a long stream of triplets. These press forward with renewed urgency headlong into a crescendo, which leads them, like an errant pied piper, from *pianissimo* to *fortissimo* in a mere seventeen measures. The pace becomes breathless as the lower strings simultaneously rub bow to string in vigorous dotted rhythms (but, as performance practice of the era demanded, the short value of such a couplet lines up with the last note of the triplet). Elsewhere, the woodwinds pipe out sequences of heaving duplets, two per bar, under a slur. The dominant key, G major, rules the tonality en route to the Allegro non troppo.

It is no accident that Schubert has already established, in the introduction, the rhythmic identity of the principal motive that informs the exposition. And yet, in spite of it, there is nothing in the least anticlimactic about the emergence of this bright, not-quite-so-new material. Rather, the seamless integration of familiar motivic tattoos informs the trajectory and intensity of a work that, from this point forward, will continue *in moto perpetuum*.

This new principal theme is only a four-bar fragment, the first two measures of which, played boldly by the strings in unison, point up a progressive dotted rhythm—long–short–long—that turns on three pitches: the tonic C, the dominant G, and the supertonic D. The consequent two-bar tag, given over to triplets, reaches upward through a C-major triad. Thus, despite the visceral rhythmic excitement, the central tonality, C major, remains unchallenged and conveys stability. While the violins keep up their dotted figure, which twice expands upward along a C-major scale, the woodwinds, horns, and timpani pipe out their nervous triplets, which have stabilized into a series of repeated notes on a dominant seventh.

The eight-bar second subject has an oddly Russian patina, as if it were a refugee troika motive from a Tchaikovsky symphony. The first two bars push off in E minor, the oboes and bassoons articulating a sequence of stacked thirds, four to the bar, thus conforming neatly and without argument to the prevailing meter. The lightly accented downbeat in each of these measures thrusts the figure forward, against the arpeggiated accompaniment of the violins and cellos. The ensuing two bars of ascending thirds, paying interior homage to a move from A-natural to C-natural, are in fact a subtle variant of the Andante's second bar, which debouche into an identical rhythmic pattern in sixths.

Here, Schubert alternates the pattern in thirds, dividing them in unison between the bassoons and oboes, and the flutes and clarinets. Meanwhile, the strings, likewise shifting material back and forth, break into a motoric eighth-note pattern that momentarily modulates through D major and B major. An unexpected sforzando on a dominant-seventh chord suggests the arrival of C major, the work's home key, but it is only an illusion en route to the dominant, G major. The mood is joyous as Schubert elaborates what by now has become his favorite motive, no matter that its origin is the second bar of the Andante.

The music now yields to the churning quarter-note regularity of the stacked thirds. Here Schubert dissolves, with unerring finesse, G major into E-flat major. The intermittent interjections of the trombones wax bucolic in ascending unisons and within a velvety *pianissimo*. As the second violins and violas toss jittery arpeggios back and forth, the horns intermittently belt out a short but ominous recall of the Andante's second bar. A twenty-four-bar crescendo becomes a reservoir of modulations as it sweeps the melodic contour of the same motivic fragment into a massive triple *forte*. It is a defining moment, surveying a climax—codified by the violins, violas, and woodwinds in unison—that in less skilled hands would have been merely redundant.

Elsewhere and simultaneously, the horns and trumpets give voice to a militaristic patter of quarters and eighths on a single pitch, astride a vibratory roll of the timpani. The trombones, joining the tumult, angle upward in triumph. Having arrived in the dominant key of G major, the exposition comes to a close with a recall of its own principal theme, played by the strings and woodwinds. Astute conductors, if they follow Schubert's instruction to repeat the exposition, will indeed risk expanding the movement into something resembling Schumann's ever-so-descriptive assessment of its "heavenly length."

Schubert wastes no time in combining the exposition's first and second subjects at the outset of the development. The strings introduce the former, while the flutes and oboes assume the second theme, passing it on a few measures later to the clarinets and bassoons. The violins bear the burden of a relentless eighth-note arpeggiation that outlines an A-flat triad and serves to sustain the tension. Without preparation, the music has already migrated, at the start of the development, to yet another distant key, A-flat major. This is fortified in the bass with an eleven-bar pedal point. The volume grows steadily from *piano* to *forte* as the horns and trumpets, sticking to their collective guns, again issue a steady stream of triplets in unison while the strings below see fit to fawn over the principal themes. Astride all this activity, the trombones again assume the aforementioned motive from the Andante's second bar but deliver it *fortissimo* with considerably greater rhythmic energy.

There's a rough-hewn edge to the fragment this time; that quality may be due to a modification of the first note of the figure with a double dot, which shortens the upbeat that comes after it.

The mysterious transitional passage that follows finds the repetitive triplets now quietly appropriated by the violins as the lower strings assume the newly invigorated, now double-dotted motive from the Andante's second bar. Here the orchestral texture liquidates, pitting a flute and oboe (which here introduce a new variant that is a descent of five notes along a stepwise triplet) against the surge of the basses and cellos.

Rapidly shifting tonalities find resolution at the recapitulation, which ushers in the exposition's principal subject, in perfect conformity with sonata form, in C major. The instrumental arrangement is identical, with the strings taking on the principal theme in unison as the woodwinds and horns putter alongside with their pulsating triplets. The second subject, too, reemerges intact, but now reinvented in C minor. The tempo picks up with the instruction *più moto*, bringing all the motivic fragments into play, along with a new but derivative figure, an ascending dotted-note arpeggiation in the lower strings. The coda likewise blossoms with ephemeral whimsy, moving into C-sharp major and F-sharp minor for only a few moments before reestablishing the primacy of the tonic C major. A blaze of brass, together with the strings and woodwinds again in unison, carries the movement to its inexorable and noble end.

Second movement: Andante con moto

The martial character of this vivid work places greater emphasis on the *con moto* constituent of its tempo than on Andante. While it may fall into the traditional general category of a "slow movement," given its hierarchical position within the symphony, its agenda challenges the usual dissolution of a first movement's propulsive energy into a dreamy reminiscence. On the contrary, Schubert resolves instead to invest in the idea that fueled the first movement: the elaboration of brief thematic cells made subject to continual regeneration. Thus the pace is, or should be, a rather brisk, even propulsive walking tempo that fulfills the aesthetic sensibility we so often encounter in Schubert's music. It evokes nature, yes, but also symbolizes the myriad anxieties that articulated his psychological disposition. Just as the musical apparatus of *Die Winterreise* leads ultimately to its protagonist's disillusionment and death, so does the bleak military cortege of this uneasy Andante con moto become an emblem of both personal determination and grim aesthetic austerity.

The form of this work is ambiguous, open to several possible interpretations. To be sure, it is a march, and its ambience of military perseverance impresses itself on the listener as such, though it does so through the steady rhythmic progression of its melodic cells and without any sense of imperiousness or grandeur. Even so, given the number of its thematic strains, as well as the manner of their presentation, sonata form emerges as the most likely candidate to fulfill its categorical imperatives. What could properly be called a development section is, in my view, a dubious analysis, in that it amounts to a reprise of the exposition that neither elaborates the original material nor introduces anything new. Something on the order of a combined development and recapitulation enjoins variants of the first and fourth subjects, for the most part, before shifting directly into a coda. This Andante con moto, though episodic, might also be interpreted as a kind of theatrical overture; in the early part of the nineteenth century, overtures of that kind were normally configured as bipartite structures without a development.

The entire string section introduces the movement quietly in A minor and in 2/4 time. While the violins and violas press forward in an unrelenting stream of largely repeated (and then chromatically inflected) eighth-notes, the cellos and basses adumbrate the jaunty rhythmic design of the principal theme in unison. That theme, taken up by the oboes some eight bars into the work, spreads its wings over nine bars, the first four of which sport several distinguishing features. The contour of the melody surveys a quarter-note, followed, on the second beat, by a lightly ornamented sixteenth-note dotted figure. That leaps up from an E-natural to the tonic A on the downbeat of the third bar. To be sure, the air of determination that informs this figure results from its altogether downbeat character; upbeats, which, on the heels of a weak beat, would normally convey a sense of anticipation and movement toward harmonic or rhythmic resolution, play virtually no part in its construction.

But it is the third measure of the tune (the tenth bar of the movement) that covets the theme's crucial tag, namely, a pair of repeated, sharply accented quarter-notes that occur, in its first statement, on the dominant E-natural. Two ascending eighth-notes in stepwise motion lead up to it, but even these, modified by staccato, abandon their functional capacity as an upbeat. This motivic shard will rear its head throughout the movement, lending an air of resolute determination to everything it touches. The remainder of the theme elaborates the dotted-sixteenth motive before alighting, yet again, on the repeated quarter-note tag, which it echoes again, and against the slim harmonization of the strings, horns, and bassoons.

A new, second subject, six bars long and cast in A major, emerges almost imperceptibly and is again entrusted to the oboe. Its air of hopefulness is perhaps an implicit attribute of the major key in which it finds itself, though it is vaguely derivative of the principal theme. It expands the stepwise motion that precedes the ascent (in bar nine of the movement) to that theme's crucial repeated-note tag. As if to lend weight to its importance, it, too, appropriates the tag at the conclusion of its statement.

The absence of transitional threads thus far in the movement from one theme to another is unusual, adding something to the atmosphere of abrupt austerity. Thus the appearance of an imposing third subject, which begins with a bold advance of eighth-notes played *fortissimo* by the strings, annihilates any diffusion of intent as it intensifies the march. Schubert fleshes out this new figure, at first voiced by the strings, by combining the dotted-sixteenth figure with the repeated note tag in diminution (that is, at half its metrical value, reducing it from two quarters to a pair of eighths). An abbreviated, alternating pulsation of thirty-second-notes, carried by the strings, accompanies the flutes, oboes, and bassoons above, which have abandoned the dotted rhythm of the figure in favor of a temporary melodic effusion. This motivic consequence ascends, yet again, to the repeated quarter-note tag, which by now has become a compositional obsession. The strings and woodwinds overtake the dotted-sixteenth-note figure in unison and in advance of the reappearance of the principal theme, now entrusted to the clarinets and bassoons in a succession of quiescent thirds. Here, an oboe courts the second subject and then, as the orchestral fabric thins out and the dynamic diminishes to *pianissimo*, subtly transfers to the cellos and basses a forecast of the fourth and final thematic fragment. This new theme, led by the first violins and doubled at the distance of a third by bassoons and basses, is set in the subdominant F major. It is also a quasi-chorale sanctified by a certain regal calm as it proceeds downhill in a stream of quarter-notes from its mediant pitch, A, to the dominant C, only to ascend again to the pitch that spawned it. Moments later, the woodwinds engage in a deftly harmonized variant, in stacked thirds, of the aforementioned consequent that they surveyed at the first appearance of the second subject.

Brian Newbould intuits some similarity between this chorale theme and a melody from Mozart's Violin Sonata in E-flat. His shrewd observation leads me to a momentary detour. While this likeness may indeed be more than coincidental, especially in light of the esteem in which Schubert held his predecessor, it strikes me as fundamentally insignificant. The motivic identity and contours that infuse and so often articulate a composer's thematic reservoir rely on unconscious processes as much as they do on conscious ones, just as dreams rely, for their manifest content, on a multitude of quotidian events. One can just as easily point to the opening salvo of Mozart's B-flat Major Sonata, K. 333, the pitch material as well as the contour of which bears no less a resemblance. In the end, what really matters—as Newbould himself acknowledges—is not the source of Schubert's inspiration, or that one tune strikes a pose not dissimilar to another, but what he makes of it. Certainly, no one will argue that Schubert's influence on future generations of composers, not the least of them Mahler, was profound. But as the history of music in Western civilization has demonstrated again and again, technical achievement and aesthetic agenda are the beneficiaries of individual intuition and imagination as much as they are environment and collective social progress.

Schubert's originality is evident in the ensuing parade of the now familiar, omnipresent pair of quarter-notes of the principal theme's third bar. In advance of the recapitulation, Schubert assigns this tag to the strings and woodwinds, extending it into a bellicose pronouncement that successively punctuates the Andante's bright landscape. What might be construed as a new melodic fragment makes itself known at the tail end of this passage; it is a curvaceous two-bar motive defined by a quarter-note which, after descending from G to C, moves upward again to a stream of eight sixteenth-notes. That this figure is set atop a syncopated pedal-point accompaniment in the violins lends it a certain autonomy, but its presence is essentially short-lived; thus it does not attain to the status of an independent subject. The trombones, trumpets, flutes, and clarinets capture a fragment of the chorale theme, which disintegrates soon enough into a diaphanous spray of two opposing dominant seventh chords as the horns sound a ten-bar pedal point on G.

Here, an oboe ushers in the principal theme, announcing a reprise of the exposition. But now a puckish repeated-note figure played by the horns and trumpets modifies the accompaniment. Schubert's writing out of the reprise—despite its differences—rather than relying on a repeat sign, leads one to wonder if he anticipated the complaints of his detractors, who years later would complain about the not-so-heavenly length of his music.

After three repetitions of the third subject, tensions boil again. The sonority of the dotted sixteenth-note figure expands and then dissolves into a meager veil of strings in pizzicato unison, which carry the two-note tag in diminution.

What follows can be viewed as the beginning of the development, but perhaps more accurately amounts to an episodic opportunity for the elaboration of two themes—the first subject and the chorale theme—of the exposition. Here, while the upper strings maintain their pizzicatos, the cellos blithely manufacture a docile variant of the principal theme, transposed into B-flat major. The oboes take up this thematic cause, but for only a few bars, cadencing in A major without an iota of preparation; this sudden move showcases the facile subtlety of Schubert's harmonic imagination and compositional skill.

Only ten measures later, the key migrates formally to A major with a change of key signature. Here the chorale theme surfaces again in the flutes and clarinets, while the first violins, acting the part of latecomers, give long bows to short off-beat syncopes. Following a wistful eleven-bar diminuendo, the second violins and violas meander astride it, propelling the music forward to the coda in an unbroken river of undulating sixteenths. Here, the oboes and bassoons take up the principal theme against the sparse accompaniment of the strings, as well as the intermittent interruptions of the woodwinds, trumpets, and trombones, which twice bleat out the repeated quarter-note tag. From here a solo clarinet, virtually unaccompanied save for the lightest punctuation of the strings, fawns over the principal theme's sixteenth-note figure for some ten bars. Moments later the second subject returns, though on this occasion in A minor. As if to make sure that no one forgets its stature, ten of the last eleven bars pay homage to the repeated quarter-note tag, assuring its compositional legacy and reinforcing the uncompromising determination that appears to be its message. This memorable Andante con moto vanishes quietly into the distance, concluding on a prolonged tonic chord.

Third movement: Scherzo—Allegro vivace

Though Beethoven virtually reinvented the scherzo as an autonomous genre defined by its impetuous energy and often cheeky good humor, Schubert was no less inventive. As we shall see, he exploited the genre just as imaginatively in his late piano sonatas as he did here, in the third movement of his Ninth Symphony. In fact, Schubert takes things even further: such is the breadth and density of this Scherzo that it is also, in performances that respect the repeats, the longest movement in all his symphonies.

Wasting no time, Schubert establishes gravitas from the very first note of the A section, where the principal subject endears itself to the entire string section in octave unisons. It is a vigorous, even ribald tune in C major that juxtaposes one bar of closely drawn staccato eighth-notes on G and A aside three quarter-notes in the following bar. The latter survey, with uncompromising determination, the identical pitch on C. This pattern is repeated in the following two bars, though here the last four eighths of the third bar travel northward to a prolonged E-natural. The oboes and flutes grab the figure, passing it between themselves while the horns and timpani bleep out timorously below. The woodwinds flirt with B-flat major before the strings return, their unisons intact, only to join forces with the woodwinds in a shrewd migration to the dominant cadence on G.

Like a gentle breeze, the four-bar second subject emerges. It is a graceful, woodsy, and curvaceous ländler—an alpine song, if you will—which is defined by an ascending D-major arpeggio set forth as a lyrical trochee (a half-note followed by a quarter-note). While the clarinets and bassoons continue to pursue the principal subject, this new figure tapers off in the fourth bar, descending to the dominant pitch, D, in a gentle array of eighths. Only two bars later, the cellos assume this appealing waltzlike tune in imitation and engage the violins in a playful game of "catch that tune." The full string section then joins forces again in unison, elaborating the second subject, while the woodwinds pursue the principal theme above.

The strings again prevail at the outset of the B section, but they are now enriched and harmonized by the woodwinds and brass, which stay afloat, for some eight bars, over a prolonged A-flat major triad. Within moments the cellos give voice to a new theme, an effusive, long-limbed variant of the second subject, stretching some nine bars.

The principal subject never falls from view even here but alternates blithely between the upper strings and the woodwinds, save for the flutes. But the flutes have not exactly gone on holiday; on the contrary, they pursue an entirely new theme astride the subtle oscillating accompaniment of the clarinets and bassoons. Cast in the remote key of C-flat major, this tune is a lyrical profusion of descending quarter-notes in stepwise motion. The second violins and violas provide a jolly accompaniment in quarter-notes, prominently accentuating the third beat of each of the next sixteen bars. The first violins, doubled by an oboe, then take over this new theme, shifting the tonality to C major. As the woodwinds and brass likewise punch out third-beat sforzandos, the strings regroup, again in unison, with the principal subject. That done, the soulful, roundabout arpeggiations of the second subject reemerge. They are intensified yet again by the strings in unison as the woodwinds relentlessly engage of the audacious principal subject. The dynamic widens, debouching onto a boisterous *fortissimo*.

At last, the principal thematic material of the A section surfaces for restatement, though it now configures itself anew. The principal theme is no longer arranged in a stern unison pronouncement given over entirely to the strings. Instead, it resumes its business quietly, now dividing itself lightly among the strings in intermittent imitation. A terse coda incorporates all the motivic material thus far, including the cellos' suave B-section variant of the second subject.

The horns usher in the ensuing trio quietly, lending their soft brass to a single pitch, E, the dominant of the new key, A major. This figure, which here extends for eight bars, is nothing more than a prolonged variant of the three repeated notes that form the second bar of the Scherzo's principal subject. The clarinets, oboes, and trombones join the horns moments later in advance of the presentation of the trio's principal theme. Here, the violins, violas, and cellos survey the accompaniment, an arpeggiated figure that owes its design to the Scherzo's second subject. The woodwinds now assume responsibility for the songful new theme, the thematic design of which is not unlike the transitory third theme in the Scherzo. Again, it is an alpine lied dignified by a certain *schwung* ("swing") that codifies the ebb and flow from short note values (quarters) to a long one (a D-major triad prolonged over three bars). The latter proceeds in stacked thirds in the flutes and oboes, while the clarinets splay out with open fifths. This evocation of the countryside yields its patina and perspective with all the color and depth of a Corot landscape. As always, Schubert finds an ingenious route to an alternative key, bringing the first section of the trio to a close in C-sharp minor.

The second section of the trio begins in A major. It is no less rich or playful, inaugurating as it does a new period of the trio's principal theme, which, though again entrusted to the woodwinds, is somewhat busier than its compatriot. Here a procession of thirds and sixths in quarter-note motion are gently chided by the rocking motion of an accompanying dactyl, played by the horns, on the dominant pitch, E. Only ten bars later, the tonality shifts again, this time to A minor, then to C major. Unsatisfied with its tonal status, the trio's principal theme emerges again in A major, takes a momentary side trip to B-flat major, and finally alights again in A major en route to the traditional repeat of the Scherzo. The movement draws to its conclusion in A major in preparation for the splendors to come in the finale.

Fourth movement: Allegro vivace

The headlong rush into this blistering finale, played in 2/4 time by all three instrumental groups in unison, is a fanfare of sorts. At first, the function of this unusually energetic material is vague, in that the declamative yet fragmentary character of the figure suggests it might be only a onetime affair, as if it were an introduction to something more Schubertian and melodious. But to expect any such thing is to rely on rumor and to buy into the litany of clichés that for more than a hundred years pigeonholed poor Schubert as a midwife to innocuous and charming melodies.

This opening figure, for all its rhetorical bluster, prevails for some time. Its identity relies on its articulate rhythmic profile, and it is indeed the first theme of this bubbly exposition. Occupying a four-bar phrase period that flies by in seconds, it comprises a brusque dotted-note figure (a dotted eighth-note followed by a sixteenth) that ascends immediately to a crisply accented whole-note, only to be steadied, moments later, by a no-less-anxious triplet and another prolonged, accented downbeat. For all that, the figure definitively establishes C major as the key and refuses to stray from it. Schubert's placement of such absolute confidence in the movement's central tonality without so much as straying, even for a moment, to even a single nonharmonic pitch may be construed as a surprise in its own right. Evidently he wanted absolutely nothing to muddy the harmonic waters. Following a repetition of this opening subject, an aggressive parade of triplets, carried by the strings, takes charge. Indeed, the woodwinds and brass have dropped out of sight altogether, at least temporarily.

With the dotted-note figure in tow, the woodwinds and brass assume their place again in a *fortissimo* fury of prolonged sforzandos and buzzing trills. Four rapidly descending sixteenths, given over to the flutes, oboes, clarinets, and first violins, alight on the tonic, then do so again a few bars later. Here the violins tweak their triplets as the oboes and bassoons saunter legato through a descending and then ascending sequence of chromatically inflected parallel thirds. Meanwhile, the violas, cellos, and basses maintain tension by clinging to a long pedal point for nearly twenty-six measures. The violins pursue their triplet pattern into a higher register, buzzing breathlessly in unison until the woodwinds marshal their collective forces with uncompromising fortitude and proudly proclaim the parade of thirds. The horns, too, double up as they echo the dotted figure atop the trombones and a threatening rumble of timpani.

The strings and winds hang on to the figure, extending it further, giving way to a rising and falling doted-note scale. By now, C major has begun to doubt itself, and the introduction of foreign pitch material suggests that the tonality is at last getting itchy feet. But now, the strings, refusing to abandon the whirlwind of impatient triplets that drive the music forward with such compelling intensity, again alight on a pedal point, this time on D, the dominant of the key that now prevails, G major.

An abrupt cadence on G in tutti anticipates a brief two-and-a-half-bar silence. Here the horns, sporting four airily accented D-naturals, each a whole-note, anticipate the second subject. On its heels the oboes, clarinets, and bassoons announce this new melody, lugging it forward in a jaunty succession of repeated parallel thirds. Despite the relatively lean harmonization, there is a certain stridency about this figure; it is propelled inevitably forward by the mercurial triplet figure that continues to flicker quietly under the skittish bows of the violins and violas. Its melodic contour, arranged in four-bar phrase periods, is nearly identical to the earlier succession of parallel thirds—it can thus be construed as a variant—although on this occasion it contains a reference to the dotted figure that informed its earlier incarnation. Soon enough, the oboes yield their prominence to the flutes, which enrich the overall texture.

By now the key has migrated to the dominant, G major. But a cadence on a massive B-major triad interrupts, heralded by the woodwinds and trombone and supported by the strings, serving to momentarily throw off our bearings. No sooner does this cadence present itself than the second subject rears its head at the distance of a half-tone higher, in C. The sudden unprepared juxtaposition of these clashing tonalities is startling, but more surprises are in store. A singular climactic moment on a triple *forte*, played in tutti, thins out to a delicate spray of clarinets, oboes, and strings, slightly punctuated, by the woodwinds above, with the dotted figure of the principal subject. A succinct codetta welcomes a descending variant of the second subject, as well as a return of the first, and the exposition fades out on the dominant.

Against the ongoing dotted-note chatter of the strings, the development pursues yet another variant of the second subject, though with a twist: Schubert has configured it as a citation of the *Ode to Joy* from Beethoven's Ninth Symphony. While the oboes remain the tune's custodians, the flutes and clarinets, moving apart from each other in contrary motion, survey the compositional topography from on high. Soon enough, a mysterious shudder, articulated by the violins and violas in tremolo, materializes like a vague but whimsical apparition. It is essentially a restatement of the second subject, now materially transformed. The flutes and woodwinds, in thirds and sixths, further elaborate the exposition's jumpy thematic material, pitting the dotted figure of the opening against the more fluid second subject, which here again boasts its four repeated notes like a mantra. The dotted figure, now spread out over the entire orchestra and reduced to a shadow of its former self, gains the upper hand. Now the woodwinds, led by the flutes and clarinets, assume the melodic pulsations, while the basses and timpani hold forth, for some forty-seven bars, with a hushed pedal point on G.

An obsessive round of the principal subject's dotted figure presses ahead within the halo of the horns' extended pedal point, which is likewise on the dominant G. Blossoming into an imperious *fortissimo*, the woodwinds and strings combine to announce the arrival of the recapitulation, which begins in E-flat major. Here, the principal thematic material of the first half of the exposition asserts itself anew, just as it should in sonata form. Toeing the compositional party line, the second subject follows it. Once again, silence precedes its announcement by the horns, which usher in this artful tune, including the now-familiar motive of four repeated notes, in an enormous 180-bar coda.

Having temporarily banished the brass and woodwinds, the recapitulation dwindles to a bare *pianissimo* whisper. With this, the coda emerges atop a prolonged pedal point on C, intoned by the clarinets, second violins, cellos, and basses. Some sixteen bars later, the pitch drops to a B-flat and then, one bar later, to A-natural, as the first violins pay tribute again to their jittery triplet motive. On this occasion, however, the four repeated notes of the second subject have been liquidated into a single sonority (a third) tied over the successive bar lines. As the principal themes are assimilated and compressed, we experience an increase of tension as the pitch rises chromatically every four bars. While the cellos and violas shiver in a long pedal point, played tremolando atop an A-major triad, the oboes and clarinets intermittently blurt out the dotted figure. Just then, the woodwinds, except for the flutes, press forward with a modified recall of the *Ode to Joy* citation, which rears its head again in E-flat major.

Clinging to their wispy, rotating triplet figure as if for dear life, the first violins proffer a D-major seventh chord (and thus make a nod in the direction of the dominant's dominant, G major). But this tonal excursion proves only ephemeral, as the same motivic material, now enriched with recalls of the exposition's jaunty principal subject, helps itself to additional secondary dominants every four bars. Significantly, as the rhythm drives the movement forward to its inexorable conclusion, the music seduces the listener with traces of D major, A major, and B-flat major en route back to the omnipresent tonic, C major.

Here, at the movement's penultimate moment, a climax builds to gigantic proportions; the proud and blustery four repeated notes that define the second subject interrupt the texture no fewer than seven times and culminate in a triple *forte* enjoined by tutti. Even here Schubert's motivic and textural consistency yields significant musical assets; as the woodwinds and brass pay tribute to the melodious contours of the second subject, the violins remain relentless in their command of both the ongoing dotted-note and triplet figures. C major prevails as the movement comes to a glorious conclusion astride alternating blurts, borne aloft by the woodwinds and brass, of the movement's principal dotted-note subject.

The "Wanderer" Fantasy, Op. 15, D. 760

When Georg Philipp Schmidt von Lübeck (1766–1849) penned what would arguably become his most famous poem, "The Wanderer" (Der Wanderer), he could not have known the extraordinary fate awaiting it. That Schubert took the poem's lofty, if perhaps fatalistic, sentiments to heart and immortalized Schmidt von Lübeck's poignant lament isolation and yearning says more about the composer than it does about the erudite poet. While Schmidt von Lübeck made a comfortable living as a doctor, a lawyer, and finally, a banker, Schubert, who was hardly unknown or destitute, as myth would have it, struggled for the acclaim he deserved. Legend has it that he also struggled valiantly to play the "Wanderer" Fantasy, a work well known to this day for its thorny technical challenges. "Let the devil play it," he is said to have complained. "I cannot!"

As we have seen, Schubert had long since cultivated a private fantasy that he allowed to blossom secretly. This fantasy proceeded directly from the ethos of the idealized protagonist of Schmidt von Lübeck's "Wanderer," only to be reinforced, in the years preceding his death, by Wilhelm Müller's likewise exiled journeyman of the *Winterreise*. Despite the genuine friendship he enjoyed with those who loved, admired, and supported him, Schubert cultivated, like a whispered intimacy, a darker side of his personality. In the household of psychoanalysis, does his conviction that he was a stranger (*Fremdling*), forever condemned to a fate unfulfilled, accede to the level of pathological behavior? It certainly suggests depression, and given the blindness or refusal of the society in which he lived to appreciate his genius, much less reward it, a depressed mood is understandable.

Indeed, Schubert's self-image was something wholly different than the cheerful, diligent, and loyal persona he chose to reveal to those who knew him. By 1822, when he composed the "Wanderer" Fantasy, his friends had, in effect, become his family. His familial roots were strained first by the death of his mother in 1812, while his taskmaster father, in whose employ Schubert had labored as a music instructor, was eager for his son to have a *real* job. The subsequent rupture between them served to anticipate his Bohemian lifestyle, a manner of existence that provided him with only superficial satisfaction. Here was an artist whose greatest achievements were dismissed not only by the music industry, but also by the public. Thus did he surround himself, much like a character out of Mürger's *Scènes de la vie de bohème* (and later Puccini's opera), with likeminded, if often more well-heeled, friends who became, in effect, the only family he really had, his devoted brother Ferdinand notwithstanding.

In 1822 Schubert, his hopes high and his expectations heady, had every reason to envision a bright future. He composed the "Wanderer" Fantasy, inspired by his song of the same name, "The Wanderer," D. 489, on the heels of the "Unfinished" Symphony. Illness likely played no part in the surge of his creative energy; if he had already contracted syphilis, as the evidence suggests, he didn't know it yet. On the contrary, he had everything to live for and much to look forward to. As noted earlier, the success of "Erlkönig" in March of the previous year failed to disavow the public, the press, and even his colleagues of the notion that he was essentially a small-scale composer whose talents were best suited to lieder. Perhaps, then, armed with new prospects and increased interest from bona fide publishers in his other works, something of a renewed confidence allowed him to pour himself into the "Wanderer" Fantasy's composition.

The "Wanderer" Fantasy was, for Schubert and the rest of the world, a seminal achievement that set new compositional precedents. This work belied its name, as it was, for all intents and purposes, a piano sonata, or perhaps more accurately, a symphony for piano. But in the "Wanderer" Fantasy, Schubert elaborated the fundamental elements of a new compositional process: thematic transformation. That idea profoundly influenced the music of generations of composers to follow, not the least of whom were Liszt and Brahms.

Even so, the "Wanderer" Fantasy is not, strictly speaking, a poster child for thematic transformation, wherein thematic material, upon each subsequent appearance, is radically altered, harmonically and rhythmically enhanced in varying contexts; indeed, in the world of thematic transformation, themes attain to autonomy to such a degree as to become nearly unrecognizable. But in the "Wanderer," Schubert never strays far from home (which is ironic, perhaps, given the philosophical agenda that underlies it) as the principal motives invariably retain their overall shape and identity. While Schubert may vary a given theme at any time with ingenious panache, he never abandons its immanent design or harmonic identity. Instead, he draws attention to the relationship that each newly minted subject has to its predecessor and to what follows.

The "Wanderer" Fantasy, then, is a cyclical form, in that its abundance of melodies, set forth from the outset, are constantly recycled, making themselves known in every movement. Thus the complex elaboration or variance of thematic material for its own sake, from this perspective, is perhaps less significant than its expansion and presentation in differing contexts, both tonal and formal.

What distinguishes the "Wanderer" Fantasy from later examples (and stricter interpretations) of thematic transformation, such as the Liszt B Minor Sonata, composed some thirty years later, is a matter of approach. While Liszt, in his sonata, transformed virtually every motivic cell into something wholly new and effusive as he manipulated rhythms and altered harmonic schemata, Schubert concerned himself with the unfolding over time of what amounts, in the "Wanderer," to a single motivic idea. Schubert *wants* us to hear its close motivic and harmonic relationship to his song "The Wanderer," D. 489 (which ought not to be confused with his later song of the same name, set to a text of Schlegel).

Of course, it is no less important to pay homage to the fantasy as a form in its own right. By the early nineteenth century the fantasy (or fantasia) as such had long played a legitimate and significant role in musical aesthetics, with roots going back to the sixteenth century. Originally, in the music of C. P. E Bach, for example, the fantasy had been viewed as nothing more than a kind of grand improvisation given to extremes of rhythm, harmony, and polyphony. Fantasy was a free style of composition, though hardly one that gave composers license to dismiss discipline or aesthetic purpose. Rather, the fantasy was a musical vehicle that allowed composers to challenge convention and extrapolate what was artful from art. The fantasy, as such, was the birthplace of virtuosity.

By the turn of the nineteenth century, the fantasy had become just that: an opportunity for imaginative composers and skilled performers to strut their technical wares. Often availing itself of popular tunes and dance music, it developed a reputation as a form within which a composer could elaborate any number of ideas, connecting these one to the other throughout a work. Anything was game, including the abundant variety of tunes that popular operas of the day made famous. It was a very short road from the instrumental fantasy to the operatic paraphrase, for example. Indeed, the compositional opportunities that the fantasy provided a composer were alluring, in that the genre itself legitimized, in aesthetic categories, subjective musical experience. If a piano sonata or symphony was expected to convey meaning on its own, strictly compositional terms, thus satisfying its own concept as an object of aesthetic contemplation, the fantasy had no such obligation, at least in the public's eye.

While a well-composed fantasy could easily attain to autonomy and musical complexity, it also served a nonmusical agenda. To an extent greater than any other musical form, the purpose of the fantasy genre was to evoke the sounds and sights of nature, or embody patriotic sentiment—or any elevated state of consciousness capable of shifting the listener's focus away from the grim, day-to-day exigencies of living, to a world of hopes and dreams. Keep in mind, too, that in early nineteenth-century Europe, and perhaps nowhere more so than in Vienna, life was dangerous. Disease was everywhere, cholera was rampant, hospitals were few, and medical treatments were primitive at best. Life expectancy was short. Even the smallest incident, whether an insect bite or food poisoning, could lead to premature death in a city where even the water supply was compromised, and everyone knew it. Thus the very idea of fantasy appealed to the general population in ways that today might seem exaggerated. But for the nineteenth-century urban dweller, it assumed far greater significance, in that musical experience, through the fantasy in particular, became an ersatz excursion into bliss, hope for a reasonably long life, and contentment. If the average consumer was not sufficiently well-heeled to purchase or visit a country estate, replete with servants, good foods, and gilded carriages, the fantasy offered the next best thing: vicarious wish fulfillment.

The "Wanderer" Fantasy conforms to the superficial elements of the concept of a fantasy, at least of the musical variety. Although, as we shall see, it shares, distributes, and recycles its thematic materials liberally throughout its four connected movements, it also respects sonata form. Whereas a fantasy proper could dismiss, without fear of critical disparagement, a development section in favor of free variation or, later, thematic transformation, the "Wanderer" avails itself, on a large scale, of the conventions of sonata form.

Schubert brought the weight of his once popular lied "Der Wanderer" to bear, harvesting from it not only a specific theme, but also its key. This self-citation by no means marginalizes the extramusical dimensions that Schubert likewise appropriated from his lied. In symbolically portraying, in wordless piano music, his existential disposition, sense of isolation, and ultimate loneliness, he brought to bear something more: a point of view that a seasoned musical interpreter will strive to read between the lines, or between the notes, as it were. In order to understand the source, or at least the inspiration, for Schubert's creative idealism, as codified by the "Wanderer" Fantasy (as much as by the lied that sets these words to music), let's first have a look at its brief but poignant poem:

> I come down from the mountains,
> The valley dims, the sea roars.
> I wander silently and am somewhat unhappy,
> And my sighs always ask, "Where?"
>
> The sun seems so cold to me here,
> The flowers faded, the life old,
> And what they say has an empty sound;
> I am a stranger everywhere.

Where are you, my dear land?
Sought and brought to mind, yet never known,
That land, so hopefully green,
That land, where my roses bloom,

Where my friends wander
Where my dead ones rise from the dead,
That land where they speak my language,
Oh, land, where are you?

I wander silently and am somewhat unhappy,
And my sighs always ask, "Where?"
In a ghostly breath it calls back to me,
"There, where you are not, there is happiness."

The poem's speaker—much like the protagonist of *Der Winterreise*, is a disoriented loner in search of life's meaning. It seems that, wherever he goes, he doesn't fit in and is condemned to wander, as happiness will continue to elude him. The concluding line, "There, where you are not, is happiness," became something of a mantra for Schubert as much as it did for nineteenth-century romanticism. Yearning, anxiety, and wanderlust, then, became the virtual locus of Schubert's burgeoning aesthetics. Perhaps he saw such states as worlds in which his sublime artistic sensibility would be safe from the everyday demands of the material world.

The "Wanderer" Fantasy comprises four movements, which are linked not only thematically, but literally: Each movement segues smoothly into the next and is played without pause. While each movement extols its autonomy, it is also possible to interpret all four collectively as a gigantic, overtly expansive sonata form. From this perspective, the first movement is the exposition, the Adagio is the development section, and the final two movements are a kind of extended, if substantially altered, recapitulation. The "Wanderer" claims C major as its principal key, though its migration a half-tone higher to C-sharp minor (the key of the lied), in the second movement, sets up a powerful, if psychologically subtle, conflict of tonality. Which will prevail?

The first of the four movements of the "Wanderer" is a spirited Allegro con fuoco ma non troppo (CD Track 2) (Lively and with fire, but not too much). It defies sonata form, in that it sports neither a development section nor a recapitulation, favoring instead an ingenious elaboration of its motivic material in sequential episodes. It begins benignly enough, procuring for itself a motivic kernel of Schubert's original lied. This three-bar motive, which will emerge as the principal thematic unifier for all four movements, is a dactylic figure (that is, a quarter-note followed by two eighths, and then repeated) cast in 4/4 time astride a thick pair of C-major triads. A truncated arpeggio tag follows, angling upward to an octave on the leading tone, B-natural, and then, on the heels of the tonic, cadencing on a dominant seventh. An ensuing two-bar rest, though brief, serves to heighten the drama.

Appropriating that dominant seventh as its cue, the sequence repeats, cadencing a few bars later on the tonic. Schubert's nails this motive down with unusual vigor and insistence, repeating it again for seven bars amid a celebration of tonic, dominant, and derived dominant chords. Suddenly, the musical equivalent of a chill wind, the first of many such moments in this often surprising work, materializes. Here, the prevailing dynamic, a robust *fortissimo*, suddenly diminishes to a distant *piano* by means of a tremolo in A minor. This in turn is disrupted by an ascending chromatic scale in the bass, modified by a stern crescendo. Only moments later it alights on a pulsating string of French sixth chords and comes to cadence on an E-major triad, the dominant of A minor. Thus, only eighteen bars into the movement, Schubert has already challenged the primacy of C major.

The opening material is quickly reinstated and expanded. Instead of arresting the flow of events with a two-beat rest, Schubert echoes the tonic triad at the distance of an octave, then separates the component sequences with an eighth-rest. A torrential arpeggio then surveys a diminished chord that sports the constituents of a rootless dominant of the key of C-sharp minor, which is the key of the fantasy's Adagio. As the arpeggio settles down into a rolling figuration of sixteenths, traces of E minor give way, all too briefly, to G major, the dominant of C. The gesture is oddly suspect, as if it were tendered solely out of respect for convention. E minor here is exceptionally short-lived—if flourishes for only two bars before the emergence of the second subject.

This lyrical second subject (CD Track 3), if you can call it that, is set in E major and is rhythmically identical to the first, with one exception: a tiny tag, outlining a rising major third, followed by a major second in descent, forms a melodic fragment at the foot of the theme. At the same time, the left hand pipes out a repeated-note accompaniment colored by a C-sharp, the sixth degree of the E-major scale. The theme exfoliates in ascent and descent as it migrates to an internecine mix of B major, B minor, and finally, only a few bars later, E major. Without warning, a recall of the aforementioned tremolo figure ignites, taking its cue just as unexpectedly from the bass, which proffers a single D-natural on the fourth beat en route back to C-natural. This astonishingly subtle tonal shift, which might have proved a seismic event in less gifted hands, emerges gently and without fanfare.

Here the principal subject, restored to C major, again explodes but is now redressed in the upper registers of the piano. Inverting the sixteenth-note figure that flew upward in the opening bars, it now darts in descent toward a dominant seventh. These minor but noticeable alterations of the principal motive's contour precipitate what may be construed as a development. Now the music swells from a jocular *forte* to a majestic *fortissimo*, reaching its apex on a high A-natural astride the relentless reiteration of the principal motive's dactyl. The key has metamorphosed into A minor, and the dactyl is forcibly projected in open octaves on the new tonic, A.

Like a wild steed in captivity bristling to escape, an A-minor scale cavalcades downward from a high A in the right hand toward a dominant seventh reinforced by a sforzando in the left. A rising sequence, given voice in left-hand octaves in the bass, avails itself of the aforementioned three-note tag—the minor third followed by a major second—that rounded out the E-major second subject. Things reverse soon enough; only a few measures later, the dactyl rises to the treble, shrieking out in octaves from above, while the scale figure lurks below, rising strenuously to a tenor E. The spell is broken just once as the melodic line waxes lyrical, only to be reprimanded by the dactylic figure, now articulated wholly by the second subject's unforgiving tag. The tag motive debouches into rapidly rising sequences, now intensified by jagged arpeggiations in the right hand. Reaching its summit, it alights on a high A-flat in the upper registers of the keyboard and, within the context of the descending scale that ensues, outlines the dominant seventh of the new key: E-flat major.

At this point, what might appear to be a new theme is in fact a familiar face. Here, the lyrical three-note motivic tag that so neatly modified the second subject is again put to work, this time in the right hand and astride a fluid, continuous stream of sixteenth-notes in the left. What's more, this motive turns the dactyl on its head as it metamorphoses into its opposite, an anapest. Of particular interest here is Schubert's imposition of stress marks, or accents, atop the second beat on each bar, which is coincidentally the third melodic note of the tag. The significance of these accents, and what drives them, should not be underestimated, and coming to grips with their particular function is crucial to conveying their meaning in performance. Let's have a closer look at why that is.

That this lovely episode proceeds in symmetrical four-bar phrases is nothing to write home about. In fact, in contrast to the fundamentally asymmetrical phrase periods of the work's opening measures, this symmetry comes as rather a relief. But something subtler is afoot here. Though Schubert has established E-flat major as the key of this new episode, the motivic tag, which expands melodically in stepwise motion, first in three ascending notes at the end of its first two bars, then in descent for the last two, serves a new, or at least a clearer, function here. The theme commences on a nonharmonic tone, to wit, an A-natural, the raised fourth degree of the E-flat scale. Maintaining its familiar contour, the tag moves from A-natural to C-natural, the sixth degree of the E-flat scale. These two pitches, spelled in two consecutive eighth-notes, have so far defined only the first beat of the bar. The crucial second beat, which as I have pointed out bears the burden of an accent, ensues. But why does Schubert impose this accent?

Too often, pianists interpret this accent as a sforzando, punching out the note as if it were an opportunity to increase either speed or volume. But in fact, the three-note tag here is in fact nothing more than an *Anschlag*, also known as a *Doppelvorschlag*. If to a non–German speaker those two words sound severe, their meaning is not. On the contrary, they refer to a species of ornament that was often used in

German baroque music and that became no less routine, even outside of its purely improvisatory function, in the music of later eras. In English, it is called a *double appoggiatura*. Essentially, an *Anschlag* comprises two notes, which precede the principal, or melodic, note they modify. What's more, in the conventional *Anschlag*, the interval separating the first from the second of these nonharmonic notes is at least a third; in consequence, the second nonharmonic, or grace, note falls onto the principal pitch, which it modifies, in stepwise motion.

Thus it is no accident that Schubert writes an accent over the principal harmonic tone on the second beat, which in the first bar of this episode is a B-flat. It is hardly an indication for an increase in volume, much less a sforzando, but is instead an instruction to give gentle emphasis to its function as a resolution of the two nonharmonic pitches that preceded it. Indeed, pianists have several choices available in this instance, as they can approach the resolution from varying perspectives. They can listen to the figure in such a way as to hear the first nonharmonic pitch (for example, the A-natural that inaugurates the episode's very first bar) resolve onto the principal harmonic constituent, thus listening across the temporal distance that is interrupted by the second nonharmonic pitch; or they can give discreet attention to the second nonharmonic note (C in the subject's first statement), scrutinizing its relationship and its resolution to its neighbor. Whatever the choice, the second, accented beat that occurs in each bar of this episode demands affective but nondynamic emphasis, which the pianist can construe to mean a slight lengthening of its value.

Elsewhere, in the left hand, Schubert imposes another kind of accent, a wedge, atop the first sixteenth-note on the first and third beats. This wedge is a kind of staccato meant only to separate, or segregate, its sonority from the notes that follow, and indeed, Schubert is careful to throw a slur over each ensuing group of sixteenth-notes. Thus the single notes modified by a wedge, when heard in relation to each other over time—that is, despite the notes that come between them—become a continuous voice in their own right. And that voice is a pedal point that makes of the left hand's material a perfect example of a *contrapuntal melody*, that is, a melodic line that implicitly conveys, no matter its status as an accompaniment, two voices in tandem. Thus, if in any given performance you hear a player give undue dynamic emphasis to the accented notes in this melody, increasing its temperature, if you will, by imposing sharp accents, you will know the performer has not given the matter much thought. While such misreadings are commonplace, especially among amateur players, they threaten to compromise the work's rhythmic trajectory, its melodic intent, and indeed, its aesthetic raison d'être.

Of note, too, is the similarity of this episodic theme to the second subject of the first movement of the "Unfinished" Symphony, which Schubert presumably abandoned only weeks earlier to commence work on the "Wanderer" Fantasy. In my discussion of the "Unfinished," I drew attention to Charles Fisk's fortuitous observation linking that theme to a motivic fragment of the lied "Der Wanderer." Indeed, this same fragment, a docile descent of eighth-notes articulated in thirds, also rears its familiar head in the second theme of the fantasy's Adagio. Thus does Schubert convey his obsession with cyclical matter, so to speak—that is, with mnemonic elements the entire purpose of which is to recall and also to adumbrate motivic material. In this way he objectively codifies a strictly compositional event as an extramusical metaphor, namely, as *recollection*.

A return to the principal dactyl ensues, now boldly announced, with jubilant enthusiasm, on a D-flat-major triad. This excursion into D-flat major, though brief, adumbrates C-sharp minor, the parallel minor, enharmonically translated, which the ensuing Adagio will inhabit with such melancholy. Again, a torrent of arpeggios fills out the ensuing measure, thus fleshing out the episode and separating each successive pronouncement of the dactyl motive. The tension mounts as the music migrates into temporary tonalities, from D-flat to B-flat minor, and then to G major. A diminution of the dactyl motive, casting it as two repeated sixteenths followed by two eighths, lends a determined, martial air to the proceedings. The right hand presses forward with a rising sequence of sixteenths atop the insistent dactyl in the left. The left hand then gives shape to an impressive array of octaves, which emphasize a similar motive, while the right hand, likewise engaged by octaves, presses forward with a belligerent dotted-note figure.

The codetta, alternating A-flat-major with G-major chords, commences with one of the more difficult passages ever composed for piano.

Here, octaves come into play yet again, but now in a relentless stepwise progression that consecutively angles upward in sixteenth-notes in both the left and right hands. So long as pianists do not fail to appreciate and listen to this passage as a musical dialogue, rather than view it as only an opportunity to impress listeners with their facility and thus draw attention only to the speed of his octaves, its meaning will not be lost. And that meaning is essentially embodied by the compression, and thus the intensification, of the dactyl motive, which in turn conveys, in its eagerness to sum things up and find resolution, extreme anxiety.

Coming down off its exalted, if tense, octave perch, the music yields to two bars of a single pitch, G-natural, that quietly articulates the dactyl. In the following bar Schubert moves the pitch upward by a half-step, to G-sharp, punctuating the passage, on the first beat of each bar, with a thick diminished chord modified by a sforzando. Harmonically speaking, this chord is a derived dominant and, as such, is related to A minor, the relative minor of the home key of C major. These sforzando punctuations increase in frequency to two per bar and give way to a new dominant coloring on G-sharp-major triad. The dactyl pulsates ominously, alternating between the hands, as it draws the movement to its close, or more properly, to its segue into the Adagio. Thus has Schubert has prepared the way for C-sharp minor, the key in which he casts the Adagio. It is also the key, by the way, of the original lied and acts as a metaphor for Schubert's deep-seated feelings of isolation. C-sharp minor emerges convincingly as the key Schubert associates, for reasons far less objective than subjective, with alienation and estrangement. Indeed, it is the key of the *Fremdling* himself.

The Adagio literally brings forth the core of the wanderer's song. In Schubert's original lied, the dactyl motive (which is carried by the piano and echoed by the singer, who embroiders it as a melody) serves to intensify the stark imagery of the poem: "Die Sonne dünkt mich hier so kalt, die Blüthe welk, das Leben alt, und was sie reden leerer Schall" (The sun seems so cold to me here, the flowers faded, the life old, and what they say has an empty sound).

Indeed, if Schubert had in mind the sad sentiment of his song, then it is only reasonable to presume that this wordless re-creation, though an abstraction, is no less meaningful. Laid out within the context of a distant *pianissimo*, the opening measures, which likewise give voice to the dactyl motive, set a solemn mood. The immersion of the theme in C-sharp minor provides an edgy contrast with the brighter, more optimistic tonality of C major that preceded it. If it were possible, for example, to superimpose the opening chords of this Adagio atop the opening chords of the Allegro con fuoco, the resulting dissonance would be excruciating, even unbearable. But the juxtaposition of these two antagonistic tonalities serves the same purpose, albeit in subtle ways: namely, the codification of anxiety.

Unlike the fantasy's brilliant opening, here the work proceeds in four-bar phrases. Of particular significance is the change of harmony that informs the penultimate measure of each phrase unit. These bars are the high point—the climax—of the phrase in which they occur. On the third beat of the third bar of the first four-bar statement, Schubert alights gracefully on a secondary dominant, in this instance, a rootless ninth chord of C-sharp minor's subdominant, F-sharp major. Melodically, the soprano line rises to a B-natural, which is the highest pitch of both the chord and the phrase. But in its sequence, a harmonic variant at the corresponding point boasts the subdominant itself, an F-sharp-minor triad. Here, the melodic line ascends even higher, to a C-sharp. That it does so provides a clue to Schubert's aesthetic intent, given the source of this melody—the original lied—and its consequent role as a musical and extramusical signifier: That is because, in the corresponding passage in the lied, C-sharp is the demarcation point for the word *Fremdling* (stranger) amid the words "Ich bin ein Fremdling überall" (I am a stranger everywhere).

Adding to the sad aimlessness of this wordless wanderer—this alienated *Fremdling*—is a group of five sixteenth-notes that together form a brief transition linking these two sequential phrase periods together. Schubert uses it again only once, to connect the second phrase period to the second subject, which is effectively the first variation. Although Schubert doe not develop this figure into a full-blown motive, its relevance lies in its rhythmic design and character. Though the first of its five notes, which ascend in the soprano register in stepwise motion, is tied over from the third beat of the bar, it ever so slightly destabilizes the rhythm. Lacking the pristine symmetry of four sixteenth-notes, which would so neatly divide a single quarter-beat into four equal pulsations, it moves ahead at a slightly faster pace than the latter would have articulated. And while it could be phrased and divided into two distinct groups—two sixteenths plus three, for example—it nevertheless sports its own character; it is the pianist's responsibility to ensure that it does just that. To ignore the figure's specific rhythmic contour would rob it of its immanent identity. It is precisely the irregularity of the figure's amorphous design, as well as its refusal to conform to symmetrical subdivision, that contributes to the overall mood of dread and anxiety.

What follows is a set of variations on this theme, though even here, Schubert never loses site of the dactyl, strictly enforcing its design— long-short-short-long—no matter what the context. From this perspective, the seamless continuity of these variations, which are played without pause, bears a structural resemblance to Chopin's dreamy *Berceuse*. Even so, the ensuing eight bars are not simply a variant; they form a second subject of sorts, in that they expand the dactyl, in the second bar of the phrase, into a lyrical fragment. The genesis of this fragment is again the lied. Indeed, the text that, in the song, accompanies this gentle, largely descending six-note effusion, bespeaks confusion: "Ich wandle still, bin wenig froh" ("I wander silently and am somewhat unhappy"). There is a certain irony afoot here, in that Schubert has cast this passage in E major, as if to create a hopeful alternative, or musical doppelgänger to the gloomy pronouncement and wanderlust of the *Fremdling*. Thus does Schubert pose a contradiction that the rest of the movement will exploit.

Indeed, with the onset of the next variation, the atmosphere darkens amid an uneasy rumble, expressed by a quiet tremolando in the bass register. The dactyl simmers ominously as it migrates from C-sharp minor to G-sharp minor. Once settled in the latter key, a rugged, *forte* profusion of alternating sixteenth- and then thirty-second-note couplets, divided between the hands in stentorian octaves and diminished chords, ponders the fate of the dactyl in acute diminution. In contrast, the ensuing variation restores the quiescence of the E-major second subject, though not the key. This time, Schubert casts the music in C-sharp

major, intoning the dactyl in a broad, open-octave pastel above a gently
rolling, widely spaced stream of arpeggios—six sixteenths to a beat—
below. Perhaps predictably, the ensuing variation returns to C-sharp
minor and once again proffers its troubled conscience. Accompanying
the dactyl is a pulsation of triplets, modified by a regularly recurring
affect: a stringent, dissonant appoggiatura that resolves, on the second
half of each beat, onto a harmonic tone.

Three more variations follow. The first, in C-sharp major, enriches
the dactyl, pursuing it at a walking tempo into the mezzo-soprano
middle range of the keyboard. This it does alongside staccato accompaniment of the bass and a quiet complement of broken triads discreetly
articulated by thirty-second-notes. The next variation is a gossamer
weave of swiftly descending scales, played to perfection by Jerome
Rose on the disc included with this book. It is also the only variation
to dismiss the rhythmic design of the dactyl altogether in favor of its
harmonic scheme. The diaphanous wash of sound, posing one more time
in C-sharp minor, segues into a stunning transitional passage, which
puts itself at the mercy of frequent modulations. Indeed, this passage,
which moves upward in chromatically rising sequences, is nothing more
or less than a continuous rumble of uninterrupted thirty-second-notes
given to an exceptionally fast harmonic rhythm. Following a stormy
fortissimo onslaught of descending diminished chords—a nod, perhaps,
to the expressive compositional vocabulary of the Sturm und Drang
movement that so fascinated Schubert—the final variation emerges
in a deliberately ambiguous tonality that simultaneously combines
two keys: C-sharp minor and C-sharp major. This it does by means of
alternating pitch material in the prescient hush of sixty-fourth-notes
in the bass register. An eerie tremolando, played by the right hand, is
built around a secondary dominant (related to a remote key, A major);
it punctuates the texture, like a cold wind blowing across a tomb, on
the notes B-natural and D-natural. The dactyl drifts away, in *pianissimo*
and intact, into an ethereal swirl of sonorities.

Only a fermata separates the Adagio from the next movement, which
Schubert marks only Presto but is in effect a scherzo. Set in 3/4 time, it
is in A-flat major. Significantly, the phrase lengths here fail to conform

to the convention established in the first two movements; Schubert replaces the four-bar phrase periods, which defined the Allegro con fuoco and the Adagio, with nervous two-bar sequences. From a larger perspective, the first fourteen divide up into two periods of eight and six bars apiece. What's more, the appearance of the dactyl is delayed. Here it is anticipated with a short but immensely energetic arpeggiated figure that articulates an A-flat triad. The first pitch of this five-note motive, a G-natural, is a strongly accented nonharmonic tone that fulfills the function of an appoggiatura, though it approaches its A-flat neighbor from below. The character of this motivic fragment is decisive; it commences on the downbeat with the full weight of a heavy-footed dancer in search of a place to plant his heels rather than lift his foot. The figure is twice repeated before the dactyl makes its entrance, now transformed and rhythmically altered into an electrifying dotted-note long–short–long dotted-note pattern. That done, Schubert fills the ensuing two bars with the five-note motive, now made lean through its imposition in the right hand alone. The concluding bars of the phrase wrap things up with unexpected fervor, first by raising the tonic a half-step to A-natural on the downbeat, followed by a sforzando on a dominant seventh in second position. Then the five-note motive, now thrown into the tenor and bass registers, concludes the phrase. The stream of French sixth chords near the beginning of the Allegro con fuoco soon resurface in a rousing triple *forte*, putting a compositional period on what has already become definitive statement.

Following a cadence in the subdominant E-flat, a cascade of descending and ascending arpeggios, articulated in diminished chords, ride astride the dotted cretic, which can still claim its inheritance as a motivic descendant of the dactyl. This time Schubert launches the cretic on D-flat, the enharmonic equivalent of C-sharp, and thus a subtle mnemonic reference to the *Fremdling* key of the Adagio. The cretic becomes more insistent, its fury pressing forward with unabated intensity as it migrates to C-flat major.

The second subject that follows is a gentle Alpine song, or ländler, in C-flat major, which avails itself of a traditional eight-bar phrase. The key is an interesting choice, in that it is the enharmonic equivalent of B major, which is the dominant of E major—the very key in which the

Adagio's *Fremdling* antidote, so redolent with hope, is written. Taming the cretic within the context of piano, it yields its lilt in the Viennese fashion, imposing a slight delay, which in this case Schubert indicates with an accent, on the second beat of each bar. This is yet another instance that prompts us to consider the range and diversity of accentuation; as we have seen, accents, no matter their etiology or design as dots or wedges, acquire different meanings depending on the musical context in which they appear. If there is a rule of thumb (no pun intended!), it is this: an accent only rarely indicate a sudden, brutal increase in volume, and when it does, the composer usually adds a sforzando, at the very least. The ländler continues, replacing the accentuated second beats with a pattern of rolling arpeggios in the left hand.

An expressive leap of a diminished fifth (or, conversely, an augmented fourth, were it spelled differently) from B-flat to F-flat crowns the phrase, which then dips innocuously to the dominant G-flat. A rising sequence of the cretic, accompanied by nervous pulsations in the right hand, throws the music back into a headlong rush of arpeggios and then into a reprise of the first section of the scherzo. The ländler returns, this time in A-flat major, concluding on a dominant-to-tonic cadence.

The docile theme of the trio, in D-flat major, is nothing more than a recall of the *Anschlag* motive from the Allegro con fuoco, now recycled and deftly harmonized below with prolonged tonic and dominant chords. The left hand also introduces, in alternating bars, a drooping duplet, wherein the pitch material falls by a sixth or a seventh under a legato slur. It is a configuration that duplicates and recalls the Viennese lilt that ensorcelled the scherzo's second-subject ländler. A dark-hued transition, led by octaves in stepwise descent, moves stealthlike into a quizzical sequence of quarter-notes astride an eighteen-bar pedal point on G-flat in the bass. The trio's rocking *Anschlag* surfaces once more, in lucid octaves in the piano's soprano register, only to be taken over by the cretic, which gains momentum and pitch material en route to its full-blown reprise.

The key shifts into A minor, and tension accumulates in an extraordinary, even strident, procession of massive major, minor, and diminished chords, three to a bar, in rising sequences. The imposing rush of arpeggios that informed the scherzo returns in a frenzy as it effervescently brushes shoulders with any number of keys. A tempestuous coda harbors the return of a fugitive pitch, F-sharp, and thus renews its flirtation with the French sixths that so intensified the opening material of the Allegro con fuoco. In spite of that, the overriding purpose of this codetta is not to consolidate old themes or motives, nor to introduce anything new; rather, its function is transitional, a means to move seamlessly from the scherzo's principal key, A-flat, to the finale's C major.

As the finale, marked Allegro (CD Track 4), begins, a salvo of bass octaves, played by the left hand alone, recaptures the dactyl, now fully restored to its former prominence. Here Schubert ushers in this final journey of the motivic material in a forceful fugato, in which the dactyl, now a lean and simple statement, is the first subject. With the entrance of the right hand, likewise carrying the dactyl forward in octaves, the left hand unleashes an impressive countersubject of ascending and descending octaves in stepwise motion. Moments later, the left hand reduces to a parade of thirds, only to be followed by the right hand, which now takes charge of the countersubject, enriching its octave pattern with thirds of its own.

From here the "Wanderer" drifts into a dactylic tornado. As a whirlwind of arpeggios flies by in the right hand, the left throws down the dactyl repeatedly as if it were Jupiter hurling thunderbolts. Roles reverse when the right hand assumes the dactyl and the left inherits a torrent of broken chords. Elements of the fugato's countersubject follow in hot pursuit, only to be scolded by a recall of the edgy tremolando and chromatic scale passage first introduced near the beginning of the movement. With imperious bluster, the arpeggios sweep northward to the upper registers yet again, expanding themselves with thirds and sixths as the left hand extols the now omnipotent power of the dactyl below. The mood is more than celebratory; it is victorious. Schubert refuses to let go of the virtuosic reins as the music tumbles into a restless march combining arpeggios, dactyls, and additional recalls of the fugato's countersubject. Following two bars of dominant and secondary dominant chords, punctuated by quarter-rests, both hands reestablish in tandem a figure of ascending arpeggios. Tipping its hat to the tense opening bars of the work, this concluding material, which hovers above

C major, likewise boasts a spate of F-sharps and E-flats, thus coloring the passage in an aura of French sixths. Culminating in triple *forte*, an expanse of C-major arpeggios spans the keyboard in both directions. On the heels of four crashing tonic and dominant triads, and a one-bar recall of the French-sixth-infested arpeggios, the "Wanderer" Fantasy draws to its definitive conclusion on a vibrant C-major triad.

The Four Impromptus, Op. 90, D. 899

There is little evidence, beyond the motivic and harmonic connections that link brief but powerful masterpieces one to the other, that Schubert intended the Four Impromptus as a cycle in their own right. Indeed, they are just as often performed, in concert and on disc, as a set as they are individually. However, as Charles Fisk and others have discerned through concrete analysis, an abundance of shared thematic and rhythmic material among them proves their solidarity. Indeed, to isolate one impromptu in the enforced absence of the others not only compromises such aesthetic solidarity, but robs the listener of the full measure of their musical breadth.

Schubert penned his Impromptus, Op. 90—the first of two sets of works given the same name—in or around 1827, the year that saw the publication, by Carl Haslinger, of the first two, in C minor and E-flat major. Like so much of his other music, three decades elapsed before the remaining two impromptus of the set, in G-flat major and A-flat major, saw the light of day. Even then, Schubert's music was not immune from abuse: thanks to the puerile machinations of a publisher who extolled the demands of the marketplace, the Third Impromptu, in G-flat, was rewritten and published in G major, a key that was a good deal easier for amateurs to deal with.

That these impromptus were composed in the halo of the composer's great song cycle, *Winterreise*, is significant, and the influence of that work on the impromptus is at times palpable. *Winterreise*, for all its angst and grim conviction that alienation is inevitable, hope is forlorn, and death lurks just around the corner, was nevertheless a kind of autobiography. Thus shades of its aesthetic agenda, which elevated musical irony to unforeseen heights, informs virtually everything Schubert composed in its wake. He knew he was dying, and evidently he wanted everyone else to know it, too.

Impromptu No. I in C Minor (CD Track 5)

Perhaps the first and most formidable challenge of this expansive work lies in the identification or categorization of its form. Several interpretations prevail, though not one of them seems to stand on ceremony. Indeed, what appeals to theorists and pianists alike is the manner in which its rich materials unfold amid the constantly shifting harmonic schema that lends it its uniqueness and integrity.

Even so, it would be easy enough to elaborate the work as a tripartite confection, assigning to it an only moderately long A section, followed by two B sections, a codetta, and, as a kind of stand-in for a development, a middle section that intensifies its memorable themes. Another perhaps more palatable interpretation sets the work squarely in the arena of a theme and variations. Given the homologous character of its fluid progressions and motivic manipulations, that may be a more reasonable, or at least more workable, analysis, if oversimplistic.

The imposition of either form onto this work strikes me as fundamentally untenable. The C Minor Impromptu, one of Schubert's last and most thoughtful works, relies for its very life on motivic development and integration. Its compositional sphere is that of the micro, not the macro, in that it gives birth to small thematic cells, which then exfoliate or blossom autonomously without ever losing sight of their familial roots. Schubert spins out these cells as an ongoing narrative thread, much in the way a seasoned storyteller conveys a popular legend: with an improvisatory air guided by logic and the teleological demands of the narrative's structure.

That said, it might just be possible, and even desirable, to think of this impromptu as an early example of developing variation, itself a species of fantasy wherein structural elements become the principal protagonists of a composition. From this perspective, each motivic cell itself becomes an object of contemplation, thoughtful elaboration, and dynamic objectification.

In *Recurring Cycles: Contexts for the Interpretation of Schubert's Impromptus and Last Sonatas*, Charles Fisk intuits a connection between this impromptu and two of Schubert's darker, more fatalistic lieder from *Winterreise*, namely, *Der Wegweiser* (The Signpost) and *Gute Nacht* (Good Night). Though Schubert makes no specific citation from either lied, the impromptu shares with both the inexorable walking tempo, a grim, marchlike pace that forecloses consolation, presages doom, and extols alienation. Additionally, the relationship of major to minor key regions suggests a certain complicity, as if the aesthetic climate and philosophical atmosphere of these songs governs the wordless environment of the impromptu.

The contrasts of mood, texture, and key that Schubert imposes in this brief impromptu give way, by subjective default, to a parallel interpretation. Given the temporal proximity of the composition of *Winterreise* and the Impromptus, Op. 90, is it really a stretch to interpret such extramusical agenda as informing the compositional meaning, or at least its intent? What is not spoken is not necessarily without meaning, after all, even when that meaning is at once abstract and conveyed on its own autonomous—which is to say, compositional—terms.

Like a trumpet calling the troops to arms, double octaves on the dominant G announce the opening of this C-minor impromptu. That Schubert imposes the dominant as his inaugural salvo is no accident, as it sets the stage for things to come; it is pregnant with anticipation and uncertainty, as if to say, "Behold!" Moreover, the imposition of the dominant in such a manner at the work's opening will have important consequences throughout the impromptu. Indeed, its function here and elsewhere is that of a governing harmonic aura, if you will, to which all the motivic material and harmonic constituents must eventually answer. That single sonority, G, is a motive in stasis that becomes in effect a center of gravity that continually irradiates its presence, and around which virtually every other constituent of the work is compelled to coalesce. Indeed, G-natural lurks in every crevice of this work, and in those rare measures where it is not to be found, the pianist can be certain that something significant and wholly contradictory is afoot.

Schubert sanctifies this hollow dominant with a power that it might never have acquired in lesser hands.

On the heels of this gloomy musical beacon, and in startling contrast, comes a single, unaccompanied, and unharmonized melodic strand. It emerges giving voice to a prescient theme in stepwise motion. Though the impromptu begins with a full complement of beats, it is in fact an introductory gesture; the material that follows proceeds in conventional four-bar phrase periods.

This principal melody is distinguished by its design, which promotes three significant constituents: first, there is the upbeat, a dotted-eighth-note figure in the first bar that is slurred over to the downbeat of the next and thus, strictly speaking, includes that downbeat as part of its contour. Then, in the second measure, three repeated quarter-notes on the supertonic D (the first of which, having been slurred to the preceding upbeat, nevertheless dovetails its way into autonomy) press forward with uneasy assurance; and finally, in the third bar, a new motivic fragment comprises three notes in descending stepwise motion: a dotted quarter, an eighth, and yet again a quarter, all under a single slur. The phrase wraps up with a recall of the dotted eighth. Together these motives add up to a march. But a march to what? If this impromptu fails to answer that question specifically—though the four note Beethovenian fate motive that will soon come into play offers a clue, as we shall see—its sister work, the Second Impromptu, most certainly will.

Here, Schubert harmonizes the theme, investing its processional rhythms and hymnlike character with dignity and purpose. The dotted-eighth-note figure prevails as the music expands, rather suddenly, into a robust *fortissimo* astride a dominant seventh of E-flat, the relative major. Here the urgency becomes palpable. A cadence on a C-minor triad is deftly linked to the subdominant, A-flat, in the subsequent bar, a move that temporarily relieves the tension. But the return to the cadential material in C minor is short-lived, too, when Schubert introduces a lone D-flat (the subdominant of A-flat major) on an upbeat, thus paving the way harmonically to the lyrical section, likewise in A-flat major, that follows.

But now the litany of dotted eighths diminishes, and the left hand articulates a gentle stream of continuous triplets, rather than quarter-notes. The melody that sings out above it in the soprano register is a variant of the principal theme, which is now transformed into a lyrical persuasion of lightly inflected quarter-notes and four descending half-notes. The latter are an expanded version of the descending tag that gave weight to the impromptu's third bar. The mood has changed from one of grim persistence to that of optimism and hope. But the commitment fades as the music vacillates. The theme morphs into a chromatically inflected panorama of ascending octaves, which then dissolve into a memorable new melodic tag of two repeated quarter-notes and four curvaceous eighths. Here, the lyrical, albeit derivative, second subject sallies forth again in the left hand, to the now displaced triplet accompaniment in the right. The introduction of a lowered sixth, F-flat, at the head of a recall of the half-note tag, leads to an ephemeral conversion to C-flat major. But then, like the sun moving out from behind a cloud, the theme expands chromatically only to return to A-flat major. Here, the curvaceous eighth-note tag that informed, only moments earlier, the earlier chromatic procession of octaves now gives rise to an ardent codetta. The triplet figure pursues its agenda as a purring accompaniment but is now fleshed out and harmonized.

The mood changes again as the principal subject rears its head in octaves in the piano's alto register, pressing forward against a steady stream of pulsating major and minor triads. In an episode reminiscent of the "Erlkönig," Schubert intensifies the texture with relentless repeated octaves, played *forte* astride the continual drone of the principal subject in the bass. A persistent pedal point is overtaken by the left hand, again in a triplet pattern. A menacing coda, enlarged by a *fortissimo*, moves back to C minor and avails itself of a new kind of upbeat—a triplet that shifts onto a dotted half-note on the downbeat. This gesture, too, is familiar; it is identical to the fate motive that inaugurates the very first bar of Beethoven's Fifth Symphony. It persists above a low pedal point on C, in triplets, which is additionally harmonized by a steadily descending, if antagonistic, bass voice below.

After a transitional passage further exploits the pedal point amid pungent dissonances, the principal subject returns, but now in G minor and configured in the pattern of mobile sixteenth-notes astride pizzicato syncopes in the bass. An imposing episode follows, characterized by the imposition of the lyrical second theme, now cast exclusively in G minor and offset by syncopated dominant and secondary dominant chords in the right hand. Here Schubert banishes the three flats in the key signature, thus signaling, at least on the surface, a new key, C major. But things are not quite so simple as all that. Indeed, from this point on the music migrates to G major, then back to C minor, and yet again to C major. The ardent codetta returns, as does the "Erlkönig"-like profusion of octaves astride the strains of the principal subject that, likewise in octaves, swells up in the bass.

None of this promises any relief to the strange, wordless wanderer who seems to inhabit all of Schubert's final music. The coda plays host to the principal subject, now remanded to C major, expanding it yet again in the right hand against a long and droning triplet pedal point on the dominant G in the left. That G prevails, just as it promised, refusing to abandon its dominion. Brief excursions into G and E-flat fail to dissuade the G pedal, though a B-flat, the dominant of the mediant, E-flat, temporarily usurps it. Meanwhile, the right hand gives voice to a sequence of suave variants of the descending dotted-quarter tag in the work's third bar. Another chromatic shift, articulated in the bass through pedal points on A-natural and A-flat lead eventually to an F-sharp—a constituent pitch within the dominant's dominant—that finally settles in C major. The concluding eleven bars bring us back to the opening theme, albeit with a modified melodic trajectory and duly harmonized in a mixture of C major and C minor. As if not to give up hope, the impromptu concludes quietly, in the piano's lower register, on three C-major triads.

Impromptu No. 2 in G-flat Major (CD Track 6)

As popular and frequently played as this scintillating impromptu is by every amateur and many professional pianists, it is not as simple as it appears. Key migration is so radical and so frequent in this work as to belie its otherwise innocuous reputation as a pleasant parlor piece. Indeed, it boasts a compositional strategy that codifies anxiety and inner turbulence to an even greater extent than the First Impromptu. Most remarkable, it does so in the context of an entirely conventional ternary form that relies on the contrast between its two A and B sections.

At first glance, what appears to launch the work is a simple E-flat-major scale that begins on a high G-natural, ascends momentarily to a B-flat, and from there descends to the dominant pitch, B-flat. The scale is configured in a swift river of continuous triplets, which at once establish the rhythmic profile of the outer sections. But a closer look reveals that the very first note of the piece is an upbeat on a high B-flat, perched above the G-natural that forms the downbeat of the ensuing bar. Though its temporal value is only a quarter-note, and its obvious function is indeed that of an upbeat, it is significant for three reasons: for its isolation from what follows (as it is not modified by a slur or an accent, its articulation is simply nonlegato, that is, it is meant to be separated from the following note); for its harmonic status as the dominant; and, not least, for its unaccompanied and unharmonized singularity. Each of these attributes recalls the opening of the C Minor Impromptu, whose open octaves on a prolonged G-natural provided a beacon of sorts for the entire work. In this case, things are not so cut and dry, and the structural influence of this single pitch on the rest of the work is not quite so imperious. Even so, Schubert leaves open the possibility of such an interpretation from the outset, as if to offer a kind of psychological stimulus in anticipation of what might occur next.

On the heels of the descending scale, the figure swings upward, like a dog wagging its tail, in a chromatically inflected circuitous pattern. It reaches up to a high C, descends by means of a scale to B-flat, then leaps back to an F-natural before resuming its scalar descent. Alighting on an E-flat in the piano's alto range, the last bar of this eight-bar phrase period again moves northward to G, where the entire phrase begins again, albeit with harmonic variants. More astonishing still is a third repetition of this figure an octave higher than where it began. That Schubert felt it necessary to drive home the melodic point in such close temporal proximity suggests compulsion or even panic; this figure percolates just under the surface of the elegant ripples he creates in this exceptionally orderly and pristine confection.

Punctuating this entire passage is a sparse, somewhat lilting accompaniment that falls on only two beats per bar. Only two single, unharmonized pitches flesh out each of the first five measures, and these coincide, respectively, on the first and second beats of each bar. Thereafter, Schubert harmonizes the second beat, not continuously, but in alternation with the original pattern. While these notes may at first appear to belong to the same melodic line, no matter their function as an accompaniment, they in fact form two rather distinct entities. The first beat of each bar is connected, across musical space and time, to its corresponding beat in the next; the same is true for the second beats, which likewise form a connection. In fact, it is a B-flat that forms a pedal point in the left hand for all but three of the impromptu's first twenty-three bars—the entire A' section—thus prolonging the presence of the opening upbeat as it amplifies its importance. The net effect of these dominant pedal points, other than lending to the whole an underlying tension, a sense of anticipation, and a yearning for resolution (as the dominant always does), is the creation of a bell effect; indeed, underneath it all is the ominous tolling that, like the *Winterreise* and Schubert's other final works, signals a preoccupation with death. Thus all is not what it seems in a work all too often interpreted—wrongly— to be light and cheerful, to speak nothing of a suitable recital piece for children. On the contrary, it is precisely the opposite: a cloud beneath a silver lining.

Here the impromptu drifts into a new section, which we can address as A″, at the twenty-fourth bar. The swift and consistent pattern of triplets persists, though the key migrates here to E-flat minor. A descending scale pattern again informs the melodic material, now offered within a *pianissimo* hush. As the phrase dovetails upward along an arpeggiated C-flat triad in the following bar, something else is adumbrated: the pugnacious triplet figure that fleshes out the middle voice of the ensuing B-minor middle section. What's more, to indicate emphasis and a structural relationship, Schubert attaches a double stem to the first (and coincidentally, the highest) note of the second beat of every other bar; he also spells the pitch as a half-note within the triplet formation. The first of these notes thus modified is the aforementioned C-flat that sits at the top of the triad. Schubert duplicates this emphasis successively, every other measure, on a B-flat, A-flat, and G-flat. Although the constituents of the triplets that carry these notes, which are configured in descent, separate them from each other in time, they are in fact a recall of the nearly identical figure (likewise in half-notes) in the C Minor Impromptu's second thematic group. Thus does another cyclical link surface to make a persuasive case for the familial dimensions of these gestures, which serve to bind the impromptus one to the other as interconnected musical organisms. But for now, the thematic material presses forward, alighting in A-flat minor as the gently accentuated second beats collectively ascend first to an E-flat and then, only two bars later, to a G-flat. The latter pitch, representing the tonality that spawned it, momentarily establishes itself as the new key on the block.

Tension mounts again in the next eight bars, which impose in the bass, for their full duration, a dominant ninth chord of E-flat major (spelled B-flat–D–F–A-flat–C-flat). The bass pursues the same rhythmic figure it has commanded all along, with only two brief alterations that articulate three beats to the bar. Given the emergence of this piquant harmony from the aura of G-flat major (no matter how fleeting its appearance), it serves a double function: first, that of a mediant (that is, a harmony built on the third degree of the scale and that invariably poses a perceptible, uneasy, and contradictory relationship) to G-flat major; and also that of dominant preparation in anticipation of the imminent return of E-flat major.

And return it does as the opening phrase is reprised. A codetta edges forward chromatically within a crescendo, leading inexorably to a *fortissimo* climax; its apex is a high F-natural. A few bars later, the overriding tonic of the work surfaces in the bass, alongside a sforzando and a G-flat prominently placed at the head of the triplet above. The hopeful faux cheerfulness of E-flat major, now dissolved and defeated by this excursion into E-flat minor, is compromised further by the conversion of four-bar phrase periods into a compact sequence of descending three-bar phrases. A blustery scale saunters up to a G-flat-major triad, made all the more punctual and determined by a vigorous sforzando.

The middle, or B, section, abandons E-flat major in favor of B minor. The robust theme that launches this section in *fortissimo*, and that relies on two repeated dotted half-notes (which is to say a note prolonged for three entire beats), is followed by a stepwise ascent in quarter-notes. The harmonic rhythm—that is, the rate at which harmonies fluctuate—is rapid, the harmony oscillating as much as three times per bar. These in turn land, in the following bar, on another prolonged dotted half-note.

It is no accident that the mood is grim, and Schubert took pains to make sure the listener knows it, if only subliminally. Indeed, if you abstract the rhythm of this figure from its melodic counterpart, the percussive result is identical to the harrowing pulsation of a military drumroll (long–long–short–short–short–long). This is the very same percussive tattoo that, centuries ago, accompanied condemned prisoners to the gallows. What's more, the urgent triplet figure that Schubert places squarely alongside it in the alto voice, on the second and third beats, compresses the figure into its short form, which renders it even more recognizable; here the military tattoo, or the death summons, if you will, is unmistakable: da da da DUM. Certainly, its underlying psychological affect is unmistakable, resonating as it does with ruthless efficacy.

At the same time, the bass echoes the identical rhythmic pattern it originally assumed in the A section, two beats to the bar, though now the second beat is prominently accentuated and the harmonic progression is boldly fleshed out in an alternating mixture of tonic and dominant chords. Like a general going into battle, F-sharp minor takes command of the tonal field some twenty bars into this section. Only one bar later, in a subdominant chord, Schubert emphasizes, with a sforzando, a particularly pungent, dissonant clash created by an F-sharp and an E-sharp stacked atop each other. After amplifying these thematic fragments by means of repetition, the work returns to B minor, where a five-bar pedal point on B-natural in the bass descends to B-flat, thus ushering in E-flat minor. Of particular interest here is the imposition of a two-bar hemiola (that is, a rhythmic device wherein two measures in triple meter are played in the same temporal space as three bars in duple meter). That momentarily annihilates the prevailing meter.

By displacing the downbeats onto the weak beats of the bar, Schubert conveys a sense of frustration, as if he were stomping his foot or pounding his fist in protest. Three unison octaves on E-flat, dissonantly harmonized below by a rootless secondary dominant ninth (rendered even more ambiguous by its embrace of constituents of the E-flat minor's subdominant) again give shape to a hemiola over two bars; it is a moment of agony, as the harmony conveys nothing if not a painful shriek. The last four bars, anticipating the da capo (return to the A section), alight mysteriously on E-flat minor's dominant.

Following the reprise of the A section is a coda, which reestablishes the bellicose thematic material of the B section, once more cast in B minor. But now the theme rises in ascending sequences that aspire, in their fervency, to pure panic. A sudden and dramatic shift to E-flat minor occurs in the narrow space of a single bar; what informs its urgency is the fact that there is absolutely no conventional preparation for such an unexpected change of key. What's more, Schubert broadens the registrational distance between the leading melody, which is now secured in the upper regions of the piano, and the bass. But things don't stop there. An accelerando, as well as the basses' harmonizing chords, which are dispatched here to the alto register, also intensifies the passage. A brusque sequence of truncated E-flat-minor scales in rapid-fire descent moves from a high register of the keyboard to the tenor and bass. A rugged alternation of E-flat-minor and A-flat-minor chords, followed by a single dominant seventh on the penultimate bar, yields to the implicit bitonality of this remarkable work and brings it to an abrupt but forceful close in E-flat minor. Thus does E-flat major, now rendered impotent by its parallel minor, inform the work's conclusion in a key that Charles Fisk rightly refers to as a crisis.

Impromptu No. 3 in E-flat Major (CD track 7)

Not only did Carl Haslinger, who published this work some three decades after Schubert's death, mutilate it by changing its key to G major (thus compromising its immanent relationship with the other impromptus, also in flat keys), he added insult to injury: He altered the time signature, as well, from 4/2 time (indicated in the score by two alla breve signs) to 4/4, dividing each measure in two with additional bar lines. Evidently he was convinced that only in this way could the work be fully appreciated, as amateurs and professionals alike would have an easier time sight-reading it. Such stupidity aside, we can at least be grateful that the G-flat Impromptu was eventually restored to its original condition and thus the composer's intentions were preserved for future generations.

Though there is no reinterpretation from the Second Impromptu to this one, the emergence of G-flat major on the heels of E-flat minor (G-flat's submediant) is striking, as if to suggest an antidote to the earlier impromptu's consternation; this alone is reason enough both to avoid performing or listening to these impromptus as isolated, individual works. The sheer munificence of their gestural and even harmonic vocabulary suggests something probative is afoot. Indeed, in the first two bars alone Schubert surveys both keys, moving with steady assurance from the former key to the latter, as if both were irradiated by the E-flat-minor gravitational field that informed the Second Impromptu's unexpected conclusion.

At first hearing, it might seem that the placid ripple of sextuplets that inaugurates this work in the alto register constitutes not only this impromptu's driving force, but its very raison d'être. Certainly the sextuplets are more than an accompaniment figure, no matter the function that a strictly mechanical analysis might assign them. The fact remains that these continuous, arpeggiated rivulets carry within them the harmonic substance, character, and destiny of the entire work, and then some. Indeed, the melodic thread that forms the principal subject in the soprano register, and which they accompany, would be quite ordinary and uneventful in their absence. And yet, that very melody is itself prescient, and no less referential: its first four notes are nothing less than a rhythmic dactyl, the very figure that gave life to Schubert's *Fremdling* in both the "Wanderer Fantasy" and the original lied, "Der Wanderer," that spawned it. Here again, Schubert codifies his longing, sense of alienation, and fatalistic weltanschauung in compositional categories—and all without uttering a single word.

Schubert again avails himself of a ternary form here, though in a manner that is perhaps more fluid than that of the previous impromptu. That is because, in this instance, there is no radical disruption of its consistent inner rhythm, which Schubert so deftly articulates in a steady stream of sextuplets. Indeed, continuity is this work's middle name, or should I say, its middle voice: The right hand, which carries this winding river of arpeggiated sextuplets throughout the work, is simultaneously responsible for articulating the thematic material embedded within it. While it is the pianist's responsibility to distinguish these voices as transparently as possible, without indulging undue accents and, for the most part, within the context of *pianissimo*, the music itself provides plenty of clues for its interpretation.

Four-bar phrases shape this impromptu, and the first four give voice to a soulful melody that hovers on a G-flat. But the dactyl rhythm that it proposes is attenuated when it dissolves into a G-flat at a distance of a minor third below, before alighting, one bar later, on to a prolonged A-flat. A stepwise descent of four quarter-notes to G-flat segues upward to B-flat, and finally on to the dominant D-flat. The harmonic strategy here, on which this otherwise serene melody depends for its very life, conveys a certain weightlessness; in the space of only four bars, Schubert has taken us on a relatively weak harmonic progression from G-flat major to its mediant, E-flat minor; then to the supertonic, A-flat minor (the second degree of the G-flat-major scale); and finally, by way of the dominant (D-flat), back to the tonic in the fourth bar. But the phrase keeps going, wrapping up its statement on a dominant triad. The consequent phrase repeats the fundamental thematic content and harmonic schema of the first, albeit not without expanding the melody while returning to the tonic. What's more, in brushing the downbeat of this consequent phrase's penultimate measure with a dollop of A-flat minor, thus giving additional emphasis to the characteristically tenuous submediant, Schubert celebrates uncertainty.

The second phrase commences on a dominant triad as the melody moves upward, with expressive fervor and via a secondary dominant, to a D-flat in the treble. Here, two A-flat chords, absent their third degree (C) and configured as an open fifth below a perfect fourth, challenge the work to find its musical terra firma.

Only two bars later, this soaring melody alights on a high A-flat, supported below by the subdominant, which certainly earns its reputation, throughout this impromptu, as the progenitor of the so-called amen or plagal cadence. As the principal subject continues to spin out and expand sequentially on the back of rippling sextuplets, the subdominant takes over.

Let us review the work's middle section. Here, Schubert raises the stakes, returning to E-flat minor as he intensifies motivic activity. The bass line prevails and is made busier by a sequence of brusque, anxious triplets that angle impatiently upward, filling in the space from E-flat to G-flat, and from there to B-flat. The melodic constituent in the treble, still grounded by sextuplets (but now spelled as triplets), exhales passionately to a high F-natural, which is followed by sighing duplets and a largely stepwise descent back to the tonic, E-flat minor. A recall of this passage plants a trill on a D-natural in the bass; as the leading tone in E-flat minor, this not-so-alien pitch asserts its presence as something ultimately dependent and yearning for resolution, as if it were giving echo to an archaic shudder.

Suddenly, the dynamic drops to *pianissimo*, as the dawn breaks in C-flat major. An expressive leap of a sixth in the soprano, from a G-flat to an E-flat, yields an exquisite anticlimax of sorts, betraying a moment of absolute clarity that vanquishes, in a single moment, the grim burden of the pervasive and overtly melancholy E-flat minor. After a reprise of this passage, with its bass unwilling to abandon its worrisome if intermittent array of tensile triplets, the darkness dissipates as the harmonic sun shines again.

Here, the music settles comfortably into E-flat major. A steady stepwise descent in the bass, from an E-flat to a trilled G-flat, flourishes against an E-flat pedal point in the alto register; this, too, escapes the oppression of the pitch E-flat as it moves northward to a C-flat. It is no accident, by the way, that these two pitches in particular—C-flat and E-flat—compete for attention throughout the impromptu, creating a nucleus around which everything else merely orbits.

The reprise of the first section brings the work back to familiar tonal territory, namely, G-flat major, with a nod again to the subdominant en route to the coda. But the honeymoon with its past, though resolute, is short-lived: just in advance of the coda, Schubert draws the bass line down from a G-flat through yet another shuddering trill on D-flat, landing on a C-flat in the ensuing bar. There, with its tonic pitch at its helm, the key temporarily shifts to C-flat minor, a key that gives us pause; it is, after all, the enharmonic equivalent of B minor, thus establishing a certain harmonic hegemony with the middle section of the Second Impromptu. Swelling suddenly to *fortissimo*, the melodic line drifts downward to a virile C-natural, while the bass alights on an E-double-flat. These two pitches in tandem briefly but powerfully usurp the function of the once omnipotent C-flat and E-flat, thus destabilizing the harmonic environment; E-double-flat is a doppelgänger for D-natural, its enharmonic equivalent, and thus the leading tone in E-flat minor, the key of anxiety that has played such a significant role in this impromptu. C-natural, on the other hand, tends to annihilate the influence of the subdominant C-flat.

But there is something even more mysterious embodied by this sonority: spelled another way (and including the pitch material of the sextuplets that accompany it), it amounts to a dominant seventh chord in G major. From this perspective, which is not only theoretical but a matter of perceptible fact, its relationship to G-flat major is that of the exotic Neapolitan. It is a relationship that brings to bear upon a listener's perceptive apparatus an edgy, even dissonant uncertainty, as if it didn't belong to the community of harmonies in which it appears. Once this unusual event has made its point, the dynamic dwindles to *pianissimo* beneath a consoling melodic tag, drawn from a dulcet arpeggiation of the dominant triad of G-flat major. Attenuated flirtations with B minor and G minor precede the impromptu's final return to its tonic key, while a patch of stacked thirds (suggesting, in spite of their bass registration, the call of distant horns) amplifies the harmony. The impromptu ends just as it started: on a profusion of G-flats atop a stream of circuitous sextuplets and a dactyl rhythm. It comes to its peaceful conclusion in G-flat major.

Impromptu No. 4 in A-flat Major (CD track 8)

A cold wind blows over this work, which, for all it charm, articulates its fate in the motivic shiver of its opening bars. Certainly, this last of Schubert's Op. 90 Impromptus embraces ambiguity from its shadowy yet crystalline opening, which unfolds an A-flat-minor arpeggio over two bars in a *pianissimo* flurry of descending sixteenth-notes. Elsewhere, the left hand sautés upward from its quarter-note downbeat to an A-flat minor triad, thus engaging our attention with its 3/4 time, waltzlike lilt. Following a verbatim repeat of the figure, Schubert wraps up this initial six-bar phrase with a pulsation of six lightly nuanced chords, which likewise yield to an A-flat-minor triad and its dominant ninth. The latter is a piquant coloration distinguished by the dissonance engendered between its E-flat root and its F-flat constituent. So far, there has been barely a hint of A-flat major, save for the inclusion of a dominant seventh among the aforementioned string of chords. The resultant delay of what will become the impromptu's principal key—the center, you might say, of its harmonic universe—is not quite so disarming, at least to listeners unfamiliar with the piece. To unconditioned ears its modality will ring unmistakably minor. Only when its motivic material is heard in context, that is, within the totality of the entire impromptu, does harmonic tension perceptibly disclose itself.

As if looking for a place to hang its harmonic hat, the entire six-bar phrase period clones itself in repetition, alighting first in C-flat minor and then B minor, which are fundamentally identical. It is as if, in its restless migration from one key to another, the impromptu yearns for something it can never attain. Thus do we encounter, in this work, yet another Schubertian wanderer in search of belonging. The aforementioned chordal tag then expands from two to eight bars, modulating stealthily from D major to B minor and back to C-flat minor. But the chords have barely stopped vibrating when Schubert revisits the ghostly arpeggios, which now resolutely establish A-flat major as the prevailing harmonic territory. To drive home that point, Schubert vanquishes the chordal tags and holds on to an arpeggiated A-flat-major triad for a full nine measures. He also modifies the two-bar units of arpeggios, reducing them to a succession of one-bar events. Consequently, the original six-bar phrase morphs into a more conventional eight-bar period. At the same time, as a means to ensure the efficacy and permanence of A-flat major, he ties up each bar on a dominant seventh before launching into a conventional harmonic progression (subdominant–dominant–tonic) in the ensuing passage.

Indeed, at this point, an entirely new thematic subject materializes in the left hand. As the profusion of arpeggiated sixteenths continues to unfold in the right, this widely spaced melody of open fourths and sixths spreads its wings with quiet assurance. It is in essence a horn call, or the codification of one in pianistic categories. The arpeggios seem overjoyed at the arrival of this affecting melody, as if they were greeting a long-lost friend. The excitement of both subjects is palpable as the tension increases in rising and continually modulating sequences; the harmonic gears make a consequent shift into D-flat major that coincides with their climax. An excursion into a dominant ninth of D-flat major's subdominant segues into a bolder variant, in A-flat major, of the second subject, which now finds itself cast in long-legged triplets in the soprano register. But the triplets are short-lived: the swirl of sixteenth-notes again rides astride the second subject as both wind down into a recall of the earlier arpeggiations. Things calmly move into a secondary dominant seventh derived from the subdominant of A-flat; configured as a rotating arpeggiation, it embraces a G-flat among its hierarchy of pitches. That single pitch renders the chord anew as a dominant ninth in D-flat major, thus making ready, by means of dominant preparation, for the tempestuous trio that follows.

In contrast with the wistful if mercurial A section, this trio, which sets sail in C-sharp minor, bears its considerable gravitas with dignity. Its grim melody, as Charles Fisk observes, owes its existence, both thematic and harmonic, to the central theme of Schubert's lied "Der Wanderer." It proceeds in waves, as it were, as its long-limbed melody grows out of a single cell: a chromatic oscillation between G-sharp and A-natural. The very same motivic gesture informs "Der Wanderer," and also the slow movement of its cousin, the "Wanderer" Fantasy. Escaping its provisional encampment within the middle register, the theme moves upward expressively by a sixth before descending to the tonic pitch, C-sharp.

In the trio's second half, a sudden crescendo accompanies a thematic swell to a high E astride a C-sharp-minor triad, thus lending feverish urgency to its musical message. In the bass below, a reiterated G-sharp forms a pedal point as it tolls once every other bar (with two exceptions) with the solemnity of a funeral bell. But then, as if to assure all that hope is not lost, the two-note oscillation of the trio's opening theme then returns in C-sharp major, with A-natural having morphed into an A-sharp. Shifting back to C-sharp minor, the trio reaches an anguished climax in full *fortissimo*, thus intensifying the conflict between the A-natural and G-sharp. What's more, this important motivic cell is now assigned its place in a high register and made all the more conspicuous by the blistering dissonance it proffers with the booming G-sharps in the bass.

With that, Schubert restores the A section to its former glory, though in retrospect and in the trio's passionate shadow, it emerges as something affectively compromised; the optimism proposed by the A-flat-major section has been attenuated by the trio's dissonant and alienated contradictions. The work concludes abruptly and without a hint of sentimentality or regret; two imposing chords, the dominant and the tonic, played squarely on the downbeat and separated by two quarter-rests, draw the impromptu to its end in a robust and impenetrable *fortissimo*.

The String Quintet in C Major, D. 956

Composed in 1828

First public performance by the Hellmesberger
Quartet and cellist Joseph Stransky at the
Musikverein, Vienna, 1853

First movement: Allegro ma non troppo
Second movement: Adagio
Third movement: Scherzo—Presto; Andante sostenuto
Fourth movement: Allegretto

Though it would be merely a truism to attribute the blistering intensity of this work, one of Schubert's very last, to some intensity of feeling associated with his imminent death, perhaps there is some truth to that idea. Certainly, it is no exaggeration to say that the C Major Quintet stands alone, not only among Schubert's work, but also as one of the monumental artistic achievements in the history of Western civilization.

No matter that the C Major Quintet was then, as now, an indisputable masterpiece; like so much of Schubert's music, it languished in obscurity for years before violinist Josef Hellmesberger and his quartert, along with the cellist Josef Stransky, offered its premiere, some twenty two years later, in 1850. What's more, though the Diabelli company acquired the rights from Schubert's brother Ferdinand in 1829, it was not published in full score until 1853.

Much has been made of Schubert's failure to follow the more-or-less traditional model of writing, which was most prominently established by Mozart and Beethoven. Conventional part writing in the genre usually called for two violins, two violas, and a cello. Modifying this formula for aesthetic, not commercial, reasons, Schubert's score calls for a second cello, thus banishing a duplicate viola. Given the

work's complexity and its burnished, autumnal patina, it is no wonder
he sought to strengthen his musical message through an intensification of the lower registers. Even so, Schubert was not entirely alone
in his determination to distribute the part writing in this manner;
indeed, Luigi Boccherini composed more than a hundred quintets,
many of them charming confections but now largely forgotten, that
conformed to this very combination. Whether Schubert was familiar
with Boccherini's chamber music is uncertain, but it's hardly a stretch
to imagine that he was; Boccherini's works were not only published
in Vienna, but also widely distributed by one of the most prestigious
publishing houses of the day, Artaria. Even so, let's give credit where
credit is due: Schubert's Quintet in C Major, unlike even one that
emerged from Boccherini's otherwise capable pen, speaks volumes for
his inimitable genius.

First movement: Allegro ma non troppo

For all its complexity, Schubert inaugurates this, his last great chamber
work, in the most straightforward manner. All voices but the second
cello—that is, the cello responsible for the rumblings of the lowest
register—emerge as if out of nowhere, and in unison on a single note,
C. With this meager gesture, pregnant with anticipation, Schubert
inaugurates the work's first eight-bar period.

Only a few bars later, the first violin distinguishes itself with the
first strains of a melody, a simple stepwise figure lightly ornamented
by a graceful turn. That Schubert immediately introduces an E-flat in
the viola and then again in the first violin a bar later proposes a subtle
contradiction, given that E-flat is a constituent of C minor. In tandem
with the viola's E-flat, the second violin, too, alights on a foreign pitch,
F-sharp, thus giving way to a secondary dominant. This pungent pitch
establishes immediately the presence, but not the preeminence, of
Schubert's old but ominous friend the French sixth, which we also
encountered in the "Wanderer" Fantasy and elsewhere. Whenever it
surfaces, you can be sure that something unexpected is about to occur,
be it a wholly unrelated harmonic field, a sudden change of dynamics, or

an agitated flurry of instrumental activity. The sky brightens a moment later, when the first violin again takes the lead, articulating a C-major triad and restoring E-natural to its rightful place. The four instruments join forces here, giving shape to a dulcet sigh, two notes at a time, before coming to rest on the dominant.

So far, Schubert has taken us gingerly by the hand and placed us squarely in the middle of what appears to be a slow introduction; actually, it only seems that way, as tension is created through the pitch prolongation. The cello takes over, restating the opening material more or less in reverse, but now banishing the first violin to silence in favor of the second cello. Tensions heighten as the dynamic enlarges to *fortissimo*, and the violins and first cello make an impassioned ascent. Below, the second cello has appropriated what will turn out to be the most important pitch in the entire first movement, a G, which it now streams forward as a pedal point.

Here, the first violin, followed by the second violin and then the viola, sets forth a new motive that establishes the primacy of C major. It is a jagged and volatile arpeggiation that avails itself of brusque accentuations on the weak beats as the cellos articulate the stepwise motive with which the work began. This energetic new theme is where the piece takes off, as it were, and forms what can be properly interpreted as the movement's primary subject. What's more, the dialogue among the instruments emerges here with such visceral intensity as to be unmistakable, pitting the violins and viola in spirited opposition to the cellos, to which are entrusted that somewhat uneasy introductory figure.

Schubert then extends this dialogue, flirting with D minor, before expanding the violins and viola into a stream of hammering triplets, which then ascend chromatically and with inexorable determination. Elsewhere the second cello pulses on a pedal point on G, as the viola and first cello give way to a chromatic, if transitional, variant of their own. This variant, though only connective tissue, is important because it gives sanctuary to heightened tensions as it crawls steadily upward; it is a four-bar affair comprising a stretch of rising quarter-notes followed by four eighths, and then a dotted rhythm in its third bar. Moreover, this figure anticipates its own later variant, a particularly expressive thematic fragment preceding the march theme that closes the exposition.

It is as if, in an effort to achieve preeminence in a circle of equals, everyone wants to talk at once.

Suddenly the dynamic shrinks to *pianissimo* as the second cello, lightly accompanied by the first cello, falls sleepily into the E-flat-major second subject. This figure, played by the cellos in unison, is an alternation, after a long-held dotted half-note on A-flat, of two eighths and a quarter. Above, the violins pipe out a thin pizzicato accompaniment configured as a dactyl, which by now we know to be one of Schubert's favorite rhythmic gestures. Soon enough, the violins take charge of this elegant melodic figure, while the violas and cellos give voice to a sequence of staccato triplets in sixths, as if in imitation of a horn.

Since the violins took over the second subject, the lower cello seems to have had little to do. But that is an illusion; in fact, its insistent punctuation gives prominence to yet another dactyl and thus infuses the texture with a quiet but certain urgency. While it continues to hang on to this role, the first violins move into a third idea, in G major, that is in fact a variant of the second subject. This in turn blossoms into an expanse of spacious intervals atop a continuous patter of sixteenth-notes played by the second violins. The viola, intrigued by the violin's wistful protrusion, takes it up in imitation two bars later, while the first cello enlivens the rhythm with a gentle if periodic bounce of four buoyant sixteenths and a lilting accent on the weak second beat of each bar.

A vigorous interruption of prominently accented duplets, four to a bar, nearly brings things to a halt, but the first violin rises to a high E and from there falls into a river of descending triplets. The second violin goes its own way, but only for a moment, as it hints at a melodic tag picked up two bars later by the first violin and first cello, which have found common ground in this tune. The viola, striking out on its own, seems to whisper a critique of its brethren, in that it now assumes the restless rotation of triplets. Now Schubert engages in such a rapid exchange of motivic material as to dazzle any listener; here the first violin catches the triplets, which the viola has tossed to it, while the second violin, followed by the first violin and the cello in unison, deliver the theme once more.

A new figure, a procession of quarter-notes and dotted eighths, emerges here. Its marchlike countenance is amplified by the agreement it seems to cull from each of the five instruments, which articulate it in rhythmic unison. As the second cello pulsates on a G pedal point, the second violin and viola revisit the lyrical second subject, now cast in the dominant, G major. But not wanting to be left out, the first cello takes over the theme, giving the second violin a much-needed rest.

The development commences by extending this melodic fragment. The second violin and viola assume it first, passing it on two bars later to the first cello. The lower cello and the first violin have been marginalized here to the role of a watchful accompanist, harmonizing the theme on repeated notes, A and E. The march fragment that closed out the exposition scurries back for several bars and is again taken up by the entire ensemble. But it soon dissolves into a sequential variant pushed forward and upward in imitation, first by the second cello and then, at the distance of a bar, by the second violin and viola. Meanwhile, the first violin engages in playful imitation of its own with the first cello, as each forcefully articulates a bouncing, middle-accented amphibrach (short-long-short).

But Schubert is hardly finished with the march figure, which he continues to elaborate as the strings alight on it in unison, en route from G major to A-flat. As the second violins invert the figure, declaiming it within the context of a seamless legato while soaring to a high A-flat, the viola and first cello maintain the motive's original contour. The second violin, atop the second cello's bleeping amphibrach, pushes things forward quietly in wispy syncopes, played as octave double stops astride a single pitch, A-flat. Emerging from this pitch, it launches a syncopated sequence of ascending arpeggios, two bars at a time. The first cello and viola, like two hearts entwined, continue to wrap themselves around the lyrically transformed fragment of the march. But the first violin, eager to remind them of their murky origins, posits a recall of the quintet's introductory subject, shifting from G major to E major, then briefly to E minor, and then, as the material of the development repeats, to F-sharp major.

The texture intensifies when the first violin turns the march fragment into a gradually rising sequence of sequential triplet oscillations, followed in imitation by the viola in the next measure. Here, the chirping amphibrach, its middle constituent still sharply accented, plays tag

with the second cello, which now carries the march theme in the staccato quarter-notes that defined it in the first place. The second violin
does the same, but in imitation and at the distance of one bar. This
constant teaming up of instrumental forces, wherein one instrument
willfully collaborates with another, either in tandem or in imitation,
only to switch off, either on its own or with a different partner, is the
very essence of musical dialogue.

Here, Schubert amplifies the triplets, marshaling the strings to join
forces as they each carry the figure in unison while articulating a dominant seventh chord of C major. But suddenly, the first violin and second
cello, riding a scale southward along the submediant A-flat major, bring
this key into alternation with G major. At this point, the first violin
agrees to a new role as accompaniment, poking its head through the
compositional clouds in a soft rise of arpeggiated triads in eighth-notes,
first in G major, then C major. Here the recapitulation begins, returning
to the quintet's introductory subject with exceptional discretion; the
second violin is now charged with the introductory theme, followed
in imitation by the first cello just two bars later. The tendering of an
F-sharp by the first violin and then, a few measures later, the second
cello, again establishes the eerie French sixth.

Unlike the introduction, however, the two cellos, one on the heel of
the other, take up the first violin's earlier sequence of arpeggiated triads
in advance of the return of the jagged principal subject, now cast, if
only momentarily, in the subdominant, F major. Their voices now one,
the two cellos provide their support with the introduction's thematic
tag, grounding the upper strings' wildly disjunct tempest. The second
subject reappears, but without the help of the second cello, which, in
the exposition, so richly invested the figure in its tenor register. This
time the first cello engages the theme, now in the submediant key of
A-flat, with the viola. The two violins, not to be outdone, take over,
singing the melody astride the intermittent *pianissimo* pulsations in
triplets provided by the viola and first cello. Precipitated by the subtle
color of a single A-natural proffered by the second violin in the candle
flicker of a sixteenth-note, the theme and its accompaniment take a
short excursion into F major, only to cadence some nine bars later in
the tonic, C. The spacious third subject of the exposition surfaces again,

riding high above the string of sixteenth-notes, now played by the viola rather than the second violin. Likewise, on this occasion the first cello, assuming the viola's earlier obligation, appropriates the theme in imitation alongside the first violin.

With the reinstatement of the heaving, slurred duplets that segue suddenly into an imperious descending scale, Schubert juxtaposes two keys, or more accurately, given the brevity of this particular passage, two pitches, C-natural and D-flat (the latter is sometimes spelled as its enharmonic equivalent, C-sharp). The relationship between them, which is governed by the tiny distance of the half-step that separates them, has special meaning for Schubert, as we have often seen in his music: in the "Wanderer" Fantasy, in the Four Impromptus, and in that major Schubertian song cycle that we have not discussed in detail here, *Winterreise*. Here as elsewhere, this dichotomy represents the intonational friction between two contrasting and competing ideas: one is that of pessimism and alienation, which is to say, the mindset of the *Fremdling*; and the other an optimistic glimpse of an idealized but unattainable future where the skies are always clear and the sun never sets. Perhaps in an effort to provide some peace of mind, Schubert configures the following measures just as he did in the exposition. Once again, as the viola dances lightly astride a series of arpeggiated triads in triplet motion, and the first cello gives voice to the lyrical profusion that is a variant of the exposition's transitional crawling figure.

The march theme, here in C major, combines with the second subject en route to an abbreviated coda, The introduction's French-sixth-infested motive claims territory here as the two cellos echo its prescient restatement in the violin. The brusque and angular first subject, as disjunct and excited as ever, reasserts itself suggestively in A-flat major, as the cellos offer a chilling vibration across the stern of a trill. The ensuing cadence to a half-step below on G pays tribute yet again to the power of the fatalistic *Fremdling* and its more optimistic counterpart. A telling silence precedes the consoling consequence of the final seventeen bars, wherein the second violin and viola survey a slight variant of the second subject in tandem with the expressive slurred duplets of the quintet's introduction. The viola then passes the figure to the first cello, which augments the rhythm in descending half-notes, drawing the movement to its serene conclusion over a tonic pedal point in the bass. But even here, its farewell is given to momentary consternation as the first violin shapes an ascending arpeggio that articulates a dominant ninth chord. Thus does the presence within it of a lowered sixth, A-flat, establish the shady and uncertain submediant at the penultimate hour, before resolving its anxiety definitively, in the last two bars, on two successive C-major triads, played *fortissimo* and *piano* respectively by the entire ensemble.

Second movement: Adagio (CD track 9)

In this Adagio, one of Schubert's most exquisite creations, the distinction between melody and accompaniment is blurred. It is as if two pieces are moving in tandem here, occupying the same space as they unfold but articulating rather different agendas. First, there is the pulsating dialogue of the two outer voices, carried along, of course, by the first violin and second cello in 12/8 time; indeed, the metrical feel of the movement is not unlike that of a baroque courante. The first violin articulates a sequence of hypnotic dotted rhythms, a cretic of three repeated notes punctuated by quarter-rests and followed by a delicately ornamented leap of a fourth. Below it, the cello proceeds in soft pizzicatos offering the slimmest support. The mood is prayerful as the three inner voices, ably represented by the second violin, viola, and first cello extend themselves contrapuntally into a dulcet chorale distinguished by stepwise motion and, more importantly, by an air of pious earnestness.

The phrase periods in this simple ternary form are unusually long: the first extends to some fourteen bars before the emergence of a varied repetition of the principal subject. There, the first violin joins the second cello in a survey of pizzicato, albeit enlarged by double stops (chords) and then, a few bars later, intermittently punctuated in arco, that is, by a return to the bowed articulation of the opening. This mingling, in a single instrument, of pizzicato and bowing, especially as it straddles double stops, creates the impression of a third violin, as if one had miraculously materialized out of thin air.

A wholly new melodic tag comes into view as this first, or A, section draws to a close. It is a brief but melancholy fragment of three slurred eighth-notes, twice repeated and carried soulfully southward by the first violin atop the continuing pulsations of the second cello. The remaining strings, at once respectful and subdued, proceed in prolonged dotted half-notes before resuming their chorale. Certainly, it is no accident that Schubert has harvested E major, the mediant of C major, as the Adagio's principal key; insofar as the sixth degree of the E-major scale is a C-sharp, the opportunities for the exploitation of the conflicted half-step relation between the two pitches, C and C-sharp, are innumerable. Once again, the inner turmoil represented by the relationship between them is evocative of light and shadow, of hopelessness and redemption. Schubert discreetly hints at the pair in the ensuing measures of the A section, with each pitch surfacing, at the distance of an octave from each other, within a forlorn descending scale played by the first violin and then, side by side in the penultimate bar preceding the middle section.

An ominous trill, played tutti, introduces the turbulent middle, or B, section, which is cast in F minor, the Neapolitan relation. In advance of the presentation of an entirely new theme, the second violin and viola press forward in anxious syncopes and double stops, which then gather intensity as they morph into a pattern of overbearing triplets. The second cello likewise assimilates an insistent triplet figure in its lower register that is periodically interpreted by a sharply defined iamb. The emergence of the new melodic strand on an upbeat, an ascending minor sixth, cries out in heartbreak as it strains upward to a high C. Entrusted to the first violin and the first cello, it is an impassioned, woeful lament, a searing duet on the order of an Italian arioso worthy of Donizetti. It divides into two phases: the first, only two bars long, articulates this long-limbed profusion in a sequence, which, despite the upward swing of its trajectory, orbits around two descending but not adjacent minor thirds. Because the lower constituent of each of these intervals falls squarely on a strong beat in the middle of the bar, the pulse of the phrase—its inner pendulum, if you will—makes itself felt as a gigantic two. Its ebb and flow is as surly and inevitable as an ocean tide. Despite the fundamental contradiction they pose to the thematic symmetry they accompany, the ongoing syncopes below serve to move it inevitably forward. The phrase then debouches into a busier consequent, wherein a noticeable shift of the melodic pulse enlivens the precarious pendulum, which, as it lowers onto the neck of its captive victim as in a medieval torture chamber, swings downward with even greater urgency, alighting on a strong beat no fewer than four times per bar.

Then, in an effort to consolidate its anguish, the violin and first cello, still in duet, spin out and upward in a gripping chromatic procession of trills. As these segue into a reprise of the chorale, the second cello's grim iamb, now made all the more expressive under a hairpin decrescendo, threatens to cut it short but does not succeed; the duet emerges unscathed from their eight-beat sabbatical, its plea now even more desperate as the violin expands into a climax in its northernmost register. Then, for the first time, the interior strings temper their syncopes and abandon their triplets, while the violin and first cello, their solidarity still grounded in unison, reach a thematic impasse. Here, the duo alights on a single A-flat, repeating it relentlessly en route to *fortissimo*, and no fewer than seven times in a single bar. With its bluster of triplets restored to their former prominence, the second bass wrings its stringy hands in a parade of jagged iambs, tracing its destiny in the form of intermittent, perpetually shifting spurts an octave apart. The repeated note pulsations, now rendered a half-step higher, ring out one more time en route, their agony having now become abject despair.

But the chorale theme survives, its sinuous melisma unbroken as it finds its way down to the alto register. But then, without warning, it all reaches a halt, coming to cadence on a rootless secondary dominant of C major. The texture, now reduced to a shadow, is distinguished here only by periodic iambs separated by rests. A recall of the woeful three-note tag that closed the A section surfaces as the dynamic migrates to a ghostly *pianissimo* atop another rootless dominant of E major, thus preparing the return of the original key and the A section.

The A section returns, but in a wholly new, transfigured incarnation. The melodic material, instrumental disposition, and texture of its ancestor are now transformed into something weightless and ethereal. As the three inner strings again assume the chorale theme, a transparent filigree of sixty-fourth-notes in the second cello rises and evaporates like so much smoke. Before its sylvan sonority vanishes completely, it dovetails into the quiescent machinations of the first violin, which echo the descending scale, in sixteenths, that so eloquently drew the A section to cadence. Here, the first violin waxes philosophical, given over to thoughtful pauses, gently syncopated ruminations, and deftly inflected, discreetly slurred duplets. It is as if the first violin, having been abandoned by its duet partner, the first cello, has lost its way, its heart having been broken. It whimpers and hobbles timorously, pleading with its instrumental brethren to listen. But they do not: instead, they go their own way, immersed in their sad chorale. The second cello's diaphanous chain of whispering sixty-fourth-notes likewise seeks a place to call home.

Its mission not quite accomplished, the first violin finally settles into its mélange of piquant cretics, double notes, and ardent arcos, which, in the first section, so enriched the work's immanent texture. Elsewhere, the chorale theme sings out mournfully below. Finally, the first violin buzzes with a written-out trill before ascending a minor sixth to a C-natural and, again, the lyrical descending scale. The Adagio doesn't so end so much as it dissolves wistfully into pure concept; as the dynamic dwindles further to triple *piano*, it drifts into a distant realm of private consolations and hushed intimacies so tender and ethereal as to belie its corporeal existence.

Third movement: Scherzo—Presto; Andante sostenuto

This rustic Scherzo, for all its audacious foot stomping, may owe a great deal to Beethoven, whom Schubert idolized. But this work goes far beyong idol emulation to achieve ingenious originality.

Here Schubert returns to C major. The principal subject is a deftly articulated affair, commencing *fortissimo* with a vigorous upbeat. The ensuing downbeat on a D-natural in the first bar yields a particularly pungent dissonance, coinciding as it does with the stacked open fifths of the dominant and the tonic carried by each of the cellos below. Proceeding in four-bar phrases, it moves upward largely in step-wise motion, punctuated by a small leap of a minor third and, in its consequent a few bars later, a perfect fourth. A slur over the D-natural in the first bar moves onto the subsequent E-natural in the second; but in the next bar the slur commences on the downbeat as it embraces its neighbor F-natural on the second beat. This jaunty disruption of the meter is jarring, contributing substantially to a mood at once defiant, pugnacious, and joyful. Save for the second violin, which spends the first seven bars intoning the dominant pitch G in an iambic rhythm, the rest of the strings keep themselves busy and in unison with the principal subject. The viola and first cello thicken the texture with double stops in alternating open fifths and thirds, in imitation of horn calls, thus lending the work its bucolic atmosphere. Only the second cello is given to diversion here: though it mimics precisely the tune's rhythmic contours and slurred articulations, its fundamental purpose is to ground and harmonize the offerings of its brothers. Indeed, its droning bass in open fifths suggests nothing if not a bagpipe.

Having thus established its idyllic sensibility, Schubert slows down the harmonic rhythm, alighting on vigorously accented dotted half-notes, likewise enriched and harmonized in double stops, for each of the following eight bars. An unusual secondary dominant, culled from the supertonic D major, provides a particularly exotic coloring en route to its future; it is an A major triad, and as such includes a C-sharp among its constituent pitches. Already, Schubert brings us back to the extra-musical dimensions that inform compositional tension, namely, the relationship between C and C-sharp. As we have seen, that particular relationship governs his aesthetic disposition as much as it does his philosophical viewpoint.

The Scherzo's next phase brings the motivic material into a new, if somewhat leaner, light. Abandoning their double stops, the first violin and two cellos give voice to the principal subject in unison, while the second violin and viola engage in an extended dominant pedal point, here configured as a continual patter of eighth-notes. Schubert expands the thematic kernel, intensifying its quarter-note motion as the first violin sails to dizzying heights in its highest register. Suddenly, and without any preparation, the theme drifts into A-flat major, where the violins and viola, at the top of the phrase, give prominence to that key's tonic pitch. A blustery scale passage, executed in unison by the violins, moves southward as the second cello punctuates it with an abbreviated ascending scale fragment of its own.

What follows is a surging chromatic progression, which angles upward astride a succession of arpeggiated major triads, one per bar. Each triad unfolds as an aggressive battery of eighth-notes. At the top of this transitional passage, and just at the moment it looks as if C major will reign victorious, Schubert throws a curveball, alighting instead on an E-flat in the second cello and a C-sharp in the first violin, thus paying tribute to a secondary dominant. Though spelled enharmonically with a sharp instead of a flat, this derived dominant is related to A-flat major. The first half of the A section of this sprightly ternary form draws to its conclusion with the principal subject boldly implanted in the second violin and viola, as the first violin rides happily astride a pattern of ascending eighth-notes.

The previous section's concluding cadence in G major hardly pre-pares us for what happens next. A brusque variant of the opening motive pits the cellos in dialogue with the first violin, but in E-flat major. Once again Schubert demonstrates his fondness for the submediant, a key relationship that proffers mystery as its aesthetic capital. From here, the pair of violins soars upward in dotted half-notes with a new thematic entity. The figure spans an entire octave from G to G, only to descend in quarter-note motion, some six bars later, back to the lower G. Elsewhere, the viola and first cello provide a meandering arpeggiated accompaniment in eighths as the second cello punctuates the texture pithily with harmonically supportive pitch material. A consequent revis-its the figure in much the same way, though now recast in B major.

A new transitional passage engages the cellos alone in unison in a four-bar variant of the principal subject. In response, the violins and viola interrupt with intermittent sforzando iambs, as if to scold the cellos for taking off with the melody on their own. Atop the second cello's bar-long open fifths and sixths, a swath of urgent hemiolas, entrusted to the violins and viola, shift uneasily over the bar lines. They articulate a chromatic seesaw, ascending and descending in pairs as they unfold over the course of the next fifteen bars. Again, a cadence on the dominant anticipates the segue to the next event, which returns us to the opening of the A section. On this occasion, though, the consequent phrase emerges in E-flat major, as the second violin momentarily assumes the lead along with the cellos, while the first violin and viola alight on a reiterated dominant pedal point on B-flat. A brief codetta follows as the ensemble lands *fortissimo* on an enriched dominant seventh chord; every instrument, with the exception of the second violin, thickens the prevailing sonority with double stops.

The trio that follows sets an entirely different mood. The tempo slows to Andante sostenuto as the metrical organization surrenders to 4/4 time. A change of key, too, to D-flat major is no less significant, in that it is the enharmonic equivalent of C-sharp major, signaling yet another instance of Schubert's ideological idée fixe, which, as we have seen, serves to link the two keys in symbolic contradiction.

A four-bar introduction engages the viola and second cello to proffer a serene, descending dotted figure. Though it would be a stretch to call it a citation, it bears an uncanny resemblance to the motivic rumblings of the opening bars of the funeral march in Beethoven's "Eroica" Symphony. This in turn dissolves into the trio's principal melody, a stepwise tag assumed by the first violin, which is likewise spread over four bars. In stark contrast to the rugged panache of the Scherzo, this theme approaches near-stasis, orbiting as it does around two pitches, which, as you have probably guessed by now, are C-natural and D-flat (aka C-sharp). Only a few bars later the first cello joins the first violin, doubling the fragment as the second cello harmonizes them both in a halo of sequential open fifths. A reprise of both themes cadences calmly on the tonic en route to the next group, which introduces, as a duet between the first violin and second cello, a soulful new melodic fragment. At first, the protrusion of an A-natural in the second bar suggests the key has migrated to B-flat minor, but within moments it drifts back to D-flat. A variant of the previous section's dotted rhythm drives home the funereal dimensions of this odd interlude, and, on the heels of the repeat of the entire trio, segues back to Scherzo in a conventional manner—conventional, that is, as far as Schubert goes: it is nothing other than dominant preparation. On the second time around, the dotted figure flirts briefly with D major and then G major. A change of time signature brings the trio in for a landing on a stream of repeated G-naturals, played by the second violin and viola; their motivic motion is seconded a few bars later by the first cello. With that, the trio is restored to life and draws to its dramatic close in advance of the next and final movement.

Fourth movement: Allegretto

Two keys coexist comfortably side by side in this playful, even sexy, finale. Though by virtue of the key signature Schubert ostensibly restores C major to prominence, in fact the work begins in C minor. The measured pace, though brisk, ought not be fast; it proceeds on the order of a walking tempo. Metrically, it is provisioned as *alla breve* (wherein the prevailing pulse is felt as two beats per bar).

The principal subject, entrusted to the first violin, is a mercurial confection that moves gingerly from a light upbeat into an airy stepwise descent of eighth-notes. Its thematic patina is that of gypsy music; indeed, it sports a certain Magyar countenance. By the third bar the figure has already moved into its sultry consequent, which distends a rising minor third under a slur over the first two beats, followed by the weightless staccato of two additional quarters. Fleshing out this unusual six-bar phrase is a puckish figure, an anapest that combines elements of both its predecessors, namely, two staccato eighths sandwiched between quarter-notes on the strong beats. Elsewhere, the second cello provides bouncy syncopes, leaping from a quarter-note downbeat to an accented half-note on the second beat of each bar. The rest of the ensemble, save for the first violin, lends rhythmic support to this figure, duplicating only the last three out of its four beats per bar.

Here, Schubert restates the entire phrase, setting the first violin a full octave higher and its melody doubled by its partner, the second violin. Yet a third repetition heightens the tension when it converts the tune upward to E-flat minor, a shift wholly consistent with the harmonic strategies of each of the other movements. And, as if that were not enough, the musical temperature continues to rise when a two-bar thematic fragment, culled from the eighth-note motive, moves temporarily to E minor before arriving forcefully in C major.

Now that it has found the key of the quintet's birth, the eighth-note figure expands from two to four bars. The absence of so much as a single rest in the melodic material, as well as the second cello's punchy accompaniment, lends the proceedings a compulsive character. Excursions into G major and E major again exemplify Schubert's imaginative harmonic edge. *Fortissimo* triplets on an open fifth, played by the second cello, push the A section in this rondo sonata form to an abrupt cadence.

A lyrical second subject in G major makes its initial appearance here in the first violin and first cello and proceeds in four-bar phrases. Sporting the quality of a ländler, it gives shape to a straightforward melodic strand that comprises, in its first two bars, a half-note followed by two rising quarter-notes. Wrapping up its two-bar consequent is an ornamental tag, which empties out, over the bar line, into an expressive ascending minor sixth interval. Lending support underneath is the viola, which periodically issues a spate of staccato triplets, mimicking the plucking of a guitar (which was, by the way, an enormously popular and inexpensive instrument in Schubert's day).

What follows is a fanciful elaboration, twice the length of the second subject, imitating a procedure akin to the construction of a thematic sentence in classical sonata form. Indeed, here the first violin again makes capital of melody, converting its charge into a capricious dance of rising and falling triplets and arpeggios. The second violin and viola, taking on the role of accompanist, appropriate a variant of the bouncing syncopes, which the second cello rendered with such buoyancy in the movement's opening measures. Here they are no longer skittish but transformed into a mellifluous legato. The musical atmosphere is airy, sunny, and unruffled, as if the triplets themselves were the moist rivulets of a summer shower. For a few moments in this conflict-free environment, Schubert escapes the memory of things past in favor of a vision of a brighter future. That he knew it could not be so makes this, one of his very last musical testaments, all the more poignant.

Now the viola and the two cellos, one after the other, inherit the roaming triplets in tandem with an ornamented variant of the second subject issued succinctly by the first violin. A new motive emerges at this point, but it is not so new as it seems: it is in fact a loose inversion of the quarter-note figure in the movement's third measure. Assumed by both violins and the viola before moving to a mysterious dialogue with the cellos, this thematic fragment is hardly more than a sinewy whisper that slithers quietly alongside an abbreviated recall of the second subject. As it nears the middle of its fifty-one-measure stretch, hinting at G major, G minor, D major, and C minor along the way, the two cellos become bolder, intoning in unison a variant of the second subject. The texture thickens in crescendo as the viola marches forward in octave double stops en route to the restatement of the principal material of the A section, once again cast in C minor.

It isn't long before that material is transformed; the dubious rumblings of a fugato soon make themselves known. But this playful flirtation with form is merely a ruse; it is dubious because it fails to fulfill the contrapuntal demands of a real fugato (and this in spite of the limited presence of what could be interpreted as a countersubject, which owes its shape to the anapest tag of the principal subject at the movement's opening—two eighths followed by a quarter-note). Here, Schubert avails himself of the participation of the principal subject to engage the violins, the viola, and finally the cellos (in that order) in spirited imitation, wherein the motivic tag pokes its head out, in each of the instrumental groups, at the short distance of only one bar. As he so often does, Schubert migrates through numerous key centers: in this imitative passage alone, we encounter ephemeral traces of C minor, E-flat minor, B major, B minor, D minor, and B-flat major—all in fewer than thirty-one bars! An array of arpeggios in contrary motion, given over to the violins and then to the viola and first cello, flies by in a rarefied *pianissimo*. These arpeggiations cover a gamut of secondary dominants, from an obscure harmonization related to D minor's submediant, B-flat, to a full-fledged embrace of the dominant of C major.

These in turn cadence in a manner that all but obliterates the abrupt introduction to the second subject the first time it came around. Here,

Schubert expands a tag of the second subject itself in anticipation of its new elaboration and adds a bar-and-a-half-long rest, as well, framing in silence what is about to come. Yet even now, there is a slight delay. The entire ensemble breathes deeply as it slows on to a sighing motive (a half-note slurred on to an eighth), twice repeated and likewise separated by rests and then a fermata that prolongs the silence even further. The second subject, now encapsulated in C major, returns at last and is then followed by its triplet-configured consequent. The mysterious legato slither in quarter-notes ensues and culminates, on the cusp of the coda, in a muscular triple *forte*.

Now in the home stretch, the dynamic diminishes to *piano* as Schubert accelerates the pace, altering the tempo indication to "Più allegro." The music attains to a frenetic urgency intensified by a lengthy crescendo. Atop the cello's protrusion in quarter-notes, as well as remnants of the bouncing syncopes, which give emphasis to the weak second beat of each bar, the violin and viola join forces in unison to reiterate the now extended principal theme. But now, as if to extol the virtues of its final appearance, the theme extends itself in perpetual motion for some thirteen bars, moving from C minor to B minor to E-flat minor, and then, for the last time, to C major. The dynamic swells again, and the sforzando punctuations in each of the string parts serve to emphasize the harrowing rush to the finish line, not unlike the desperate pleas of the child in "Erlkönig." The principal subject again bides its time in the context of yet another triple *forte*, while the cellos engage in massive double stops and a tonic pedal point astride open fifths.

Such a tensile accumulation of energy would naturally have led to the "Più presto" that Schubert specifically indicates only twenty-eight bars from the work's conclusion. The final strains of the coda sport a near-manic dialogue of neurotic trills between the second cello and the first violin against the inner instruments' insistent reiteration of the principal subject's anapest tag. That figure, in turn, turns insistence into compulsion when, only fourteen bars from the end, it is pressed into service one last time by the entire ensemble in unison. A lowered sixth, A-flat, makes its presence known in the second cello at the eleventh hour, as does the Neapolitan D-flat, which both cellos shake out vigorously in a trill that also includes the lowered third,

E-flat—the submediant of C minor. The first violin intones an aggressive upward scale, alighting not on the tonic but instead on a prolonged B-natural, the leading tone in C major, for two entire bars. This last-minute intensification of harmonic tension is almost too much to bear and is accorded additional emphasis by means of a diminuendo en route to its resolution on the tonic, C. And yet, as if to rub our noses in the aesthetic and philosophical points he has made all along, here and in so much of his other music, Schubert ends the quintet with a juxtaposition of the two conflicting pitches, D-flat (the equivalent of C-sharp) and the tonic, C. Thus does Schubert draw this, perhaps his most affecting and complex composition, to its stunning conclusion.

The Sonata in C Minor, D. 958

First movement: Allegro
Second movement: Adagio
Third movement: Menuetto—Allegro
Fourth movement: Allegro

In the waning months of his short life, as syphilis and quite possibly typhus ravaged his body, Schubert set to work simultaneously on a number of major piano, vocal, and chamber pieces. In addition to these piano sonatas, he penned his C Major String Quintet, a Mass, and his song cycles *Winterreise* and *Schwanengesang* (though the latter is not, strictly speaking, a cycle of interconnected texts and motivic data).

The astonishing breadth, originality, and technical innovations that inform this music were nothing less than a monumental achievement. Too bad for Schubert's short-sighted publisher, Probst, who declined to acquire the rights and distribute them; that privilege went instead to Anton Diabelli (the same Diabelli whose bumptious tune became the thematic subject for Beethoven's *Diabelli Variations*), who purchased the autographs from Schubert's brother Ferdinand in 1829, nearly a year to the day from Schubert's death. Even then, not even one of these sonatas saw the light of day; Diabelli held on to them for ten years, then brought them out in print in 1839. While it seems likely that Schubert's dying wish was to have all three published as a set, the conviction that they were intended as such comes largely from twentieth-century scholars. Beyond their coinciding dates of composition, there is at least one more bit of evidence in support of this contention: Schubert explicitly put in a request to Probst to dedicate all three to another of his heroes, the composer Johann Nepomuk Hummel.

Schubert sketched each of his last three sonatas only months before his death in November 1828. Though he spent most of the previous spring and summer writing them, it was not until September of that year that he completed them; September 26 is the date, written in his own hand, that adorns the manuscript of the third and final sonata in B-flat major. The sketches are significant for several reasons. For one thing, they provide a glimpse into his approach to compositional procedure in the last year of his life, thus pointing up both the differences with his earlier music and forecasting, to an extraordinary extent, what his music would likely have evolved into had he lived longer. As we shall see, these works betrayed an imagination well beyond his years, yielding innovation after innovation.

The final version of each sonata played host to innumerable refinements of compositional strategy. Among these are the fleshing out and development of ideas that, in the sketches, did not look as if they would attain to prominence; the role played by rests and registration, for example, assumed far greater importance in the finished products than the sketches appear to convey. He had second thoughts about tempo indications, and he took transitional material far more seriously than he ever had before, rethinking passagework in innovative and imaginative ways that challenged the status quo and yet never compromised musical logic or aesthetic integrity.

What are significant are the innumerable motivic and harmonic strategies that collectively inform these works in an orgy of self-referential material. As one movement or sonata looks back upon another within or outside of itself, varying, citing, or merely recycling this or that melodic fragment or rhythmic gesture, the music assumes a stature that cannot be claimed, at least with such deliberate fecundity, by his earlier piano music. The last three piano sonatas, for all they have in common structurally and otherwise, speak to a greater truth as they give form to what might be properly described as a megasonata. While such a description is neither formally accurate nor technically supportable, it harbors some truth; Schubert, who labeled these three works as Sonata I, II, and III (an unusual choice given that he had already composed more than sixteen other piano sonatas), evidently conceived of them as a trilogy.

Before we take a closer look at two of the last three sonatas, there are a few general ideas and patterns, worthy of illumination, that they have in common. First, Schumann's much-cited remark about the "heavenly length" of this music takes on new relevance; Schubert expands considerably the length of each movement, throwing to the winds his publishers' overriding concern for their acceptance by the public. Indeed, the length, which is considerable even without taking account of the traditional repeat of the exposition, can be attributed to a number of elements. Among them is Schubert's willingness to second-guess the development section by anticipating it in the exposition. To this end, themes, rhythmic gestures, motivic fragments, and harmonic progressions are jumbled together and explored, from multiple perspectives, well before the double bar line that demarcates exposition from development.

Gone are the litany of unisons, much favored in his orchestral and chamber music, heard in his early and middle-period sonatas. Instead we hear contrapuntal complexity, informed by any number of compositional strategies: violent tremolandos and scale passages, militaristic repeated notes, persistent chromatic oscillations over two or three notes, and Alberti basses that aspire to autonomy and the proffering of what I have described here and elsewhere as contrapuntal melody. Last but hardly least, there is the masterful harmonic language that so deftly navigates its way to remote key regions and modalities in the blink of an eye. The frequent juxtaposition of remote tonalities, often placed side by side in contrasting phrases, sections, or entire movements, offers the most compelling evidence of Schubert's radicalism. Even transitional material, whether in the form of passagework (rough-hewn scales, glistening arpeggios, migrating pedal points, etc.) or a full-blown development, was hardly immune to Schubert's imaginative resources. On the contrary, Schubert exploited transitions for their expressive potential and potency, and thus as agents of expressive modulation. In order to do so he harvested, with effortless panache, any number of secondary dominants without sinking into mere cliché, an astonishing feat.

Thus in Schubert's most mature music, passagework becomes something more than formal necessity, picaresque coloration, or a species of variation, but aspires to harmonic and structural autonomy. If there is any reason for the magical ambience so characteristic of Schubert's modulations—for the lay listener, I refer to those many easily perceptible moments when it seems as if the sun has just come out from behind a dark cloud, or a cool, moist breeze has just blown in over the compositional sea—it is precisely the independence of such material that distinguishes it from that of any other composer, period style, or theoretical precept.

For Schubert, then, transitions become a means to escape the harmonic status quo at any given moment, as if the very idea of commitment—to a single key, harmony, or melody—was something ephemeral, weightless, and detachable. What better way to codify alienation than that—to wit, to express where one harmonic region's loyalty to another hangs on only by the most gossamer thread? Schubert's universe is a world of thresholds, margins. Just as we observed earlier in the analysis of the "Wanderer" Fantasy, strategies of this sort created immanent conflicts between the tonic or home key and those regions.

Thus did the Schubert of the year 1828 aspire in his music to a kind of dialectical nirvana, wherein private intimacy and public declamation became one and the same. The orchestral aspirations of his earlier piano music, codified as such by unisons, long harmonic rhythms, and terser expositions, now metamorphosed into something approaching chamber music. Though the compositional textures are busier and thicker in his later sonatas, they are also more sinuous, discriminating, and linear; the counterpoint, in spite of its complexity, is at once tensile and fluid.

The first movements proceed in more or less traditional sonata form, encompassing an exposition, development, recapitulation, and coda. But Schubert takes convention by the throat, and, perhaps in contradiction to the more careful methodology of his early piano sonatas, his exfoliation of tonality becomes kaleidoscopic as it establishes unexpectedly vivid contrasts and heightens both the substance and purpose of transitional passagework. What's more, the motivic key to each sonata introduces itself, like a gentleman caller, in the very first bar of the first movement, forecasting the design and the fundamental direction, if not the structure, of the entire work.

Let's take a look at only one of these three lengthy works, as the limits of space imposed in this slim volume would compromise any substantive discussion that would account for all three. For readers who want to examine in detail the great A Major and B-flat Major sonatas, I recommend above all the meticulous analyses of Charles Fisk in *Cycles: Contexts for the Interpretation of Schubert's Impromptus and Last Sonatas*, as his critical insights and perception do each of them justice.

Schubert composed some twenty piano sonatas, but, like the symphonies, several remained incomplete. Indeed, by some estimates he left behind some twenty sonatas, if one counts the fragmentary E Major (D. 154), E Minor (D. 769A), and C-Sharp Minor (D. 655). Another sonata, in E-flat Major (D. 568) owes its existence to the Sonata in D-flat Major (D. 567), as the former is essentially a transposed and altered version of the latter. His eleven early sonatas—if it is even possible to say such a thing given the brevity of his life—were products of his early twenties, as he composed them in a three-year period from 1815 to 1818. But alas, mystery enshrouds even these works, as some were only partly complete, and, like the "Unfinished" Symphony, were left behind as intriguing musical torsos that wanted for last movements. Even so, Schubert left plenty of clues even among his fragments and unfinished sonatas; he never failed to sketch out his motivic material and basic harmonic schema. Two pianists, Bart Berman and Paul Badura-Skoda, took pains to re-create these works from Schubert's sketches and have recorded them.

The massive Sonata in C Minor, D. 958, on the other hand, is one of Schubert's last and most mature works. He composed it in September 1828, not even three months before he died. It is the first of a trio of sonatas that include the A Major, D. 959, and the endearing B-flat Major, D. 960. Collectively, these works recycle motivic material and harmonic strategies, and their innumerable references and citations of his vocal music, particularly the songs of *Winterreise*, suggest their aesthetic agenda was as literary as it was abstract.

The germinal inspiration for this work, so consensus has it, was Beethoven's celebrated Variations on an Original Theme in C Minor, Op. 32. Indeed, the tonal plan of this sonata's opening measures is virtually identical to Beethoven's, as both ascend chromatically and in long spurts along a path of secondary dominants. Though laid out in four-bar phrases, this opening, like Beethoven's, lends a certain harmonic autonomy to each bar; thus does the phrase proceed in harmonic blocks, wherein each bar is assigned a specific harmonic function. This species of compositional procedure is baroque in its implications, in that it emphasizes the smallest motivic and harmonic units at the expense of any rhapsodic distension or development of a single melodic idea.

First movement: Allegro

Four imposing triads, two each on the tonic and the supertonic, inaugurate this movement with a rhythmic bacchius (short–long–long). Straddling the tonic pitch, C-natural, in the bass below, the unstable supertonic (which is built on the second degree of the scale) can also be interpreted as a derived, if rootless, dominant in the relative major, E-flat. The musical mood is dark, serious, and, to some ears, violent. E-natural launches a bold ascending scale passage in the third measure, and only two bars later, an F-sharp makes its presence known in an augmented (German) sixth chord. Each of these harmonic constables anticipates the role that their harmony, so juxtaposed, will play throughout the work. The E-natural, which is a constituent of the dominant of the subdominant, already betrays distance, and thus alienation, as its metaphor; while the F-sharp of the augmented sixth chord likewise competes for attention as something that doesn't quite belong. Thus in the space of only four bars, Schubert has already made a metaphorical case for his loner's weltanschauung.

Rising to a high A-flat in the right hand, a vivid descending scale flirts with D-flat major en route to a passage of considerable consternation that inverts the scale passage of the third bar astride an insistent Alberti bass. A new melodic idea, configured as a distended triad in the soprano register, introduces a modicum of hope as it proffers itself in A-flat major. Following a cadence on the dominant of the relative major, E-flat, the second subject materializes quietly and without fanfare. Here, the mood relaxes in to this gentle theme, cast in E-flat major and configured in stepwise motion. Again, Schubert extols the value of secondary dominants and distant keys, allows the second subject to play tag with both D-flat major and G-flat major. The quiescent interplay, in the context of E-flat major, of three pitches, D-flat, C-flat, and G-flat, illustrates the malleability of the work's shifting tonalities and harmonic sensibility.

What follows are variants of the second theme, which conform to the structure we intuited earlier: a development embedded within the exposition and in advance of the development proper. The first variant is a lyrical confection that sets the stepwise motion of the second subject in octaves above a stream of languid triplets; the second variant, in E-flat minor, avails itself of the identical tune as it exploits agitation in a perpetuum of sixteenths in the right hand and a lightly accented eighth-note figure in the left. A half-cadence on an E-flat-major triad opens onto the exposition's closing theme, a profusion of octaves atop mobile rivulets of eighth-notes, as well as an E-flat pedal, in the bass. The presence of a C-flat renders the key center of this passage ambiguous; it moves in and out of E-flat major and E-flat minor with facile grace.

Here, the development proper begins its journey, commencing on an A-flat major triad (the submediant, or perhaps more relevant to the larger tonal scheme, the dominant of the subdominant). Astride the chromatically rising bass, the right hand outlines a heady consequent of ascending and descending sixteenth-notes, which, undecided on which key they might belong to, use B-flat minor, C minor, and G major as their harmonic capital. A cadence. Suddenly, the key signature itself regroups, annihilating its three flats in its wake. Are we in C major?

That's not likely; a more logical scenario puts things squarely in neutral territory, as if this section of the development were the harmonic equivalent of Switzerland during World War II. From this perspective, harmony is free to roam and explore and to do as it pleases. Indeed, on the cusp of the signature change we find ourselves in D major, not C major. A cadence segues into a *pianissimo* growl of D-major arpeggios quietly voiced in the piano's baritone register and played by the right hand. Meanwhile, the left hand articulates a mysterious thematic fragment only two bars in length and based on the chromatic stepwise motion of the second subject. Like a dog chasing its tail, this eighth-note undercurrent revolves upon itself, eventually expanding its shape as octaves in the brighter registrational territory of the piano's soprano register.

But the fragment returns to the moribund bass, where it is eerily enshrouded from above in the halo of a descending chromatic scale. Indeed, this is nothing if not an ideal example of the aforementioned transitional passage having assumed a life of its own. The chromatic scale survives its counterpoint with the thematic fragment, which disappears into a recall of the opening motive's bacchius, now expressed in a sequence of diminished and minor chords.

With a swift scalar descent spread out over a dominant seventh, the materials of the exposition abruptly reestablish themselves, giving way to a variant a few bars later with a jaunty, marchlike parade of disjunct octaves in the left hand. The second subject returns to its rightful place, though now in C major, as does its octave-saturated first variant. The second variant sinks into C minor, which is already in the gravitational pull of a reprise of the third subject. Just as it did in the exposition, it again straddles two modalities, C minor and C major.

A measure-long silence, prolonged by a fermata, separates the close of the recapitulation from the ensuing coda. The emptiness of this moment is that of barren desolation, of finality, of nothingness, as if this otherwise simple cadence on a dominant seventh was pregnant with a more ominous message. The abrupt dissolution of musical material here brings to mind Nietzsche's famous aphorism "Stare into the abyss, and the abyss stares back at you." Certainly, it would have been easy enough for Schubert to have reiterated the opening chords and bring everything to a swift and sudden halt, but he chose instead to twist the knife, wringing out the last drop of blood from an already dying organism. Thus does the coda, which is conventionally cast in C minor, exploit the dark chromatic oscillation in the left hand, which pulsed so stealthily through the development. The motive is slightly varied by means of a descending diatonic tag of eighth-notes, which give emphasis to symmetry.

The road to the movement's end is paved with a downward swell of broken octaves, which also recall, perhaps not coincidentally, the fourth of Beethoven's no-less-troubling Variations in C Minor. The movement drifts away quietly and in diminuendo, from dominant to tonic, in a stream of no fewer than nine repetitions of a C-minor triad.

Second movement: Adagio

Beethoven is yet again the inspiration for this movement, or so it would seem: the slow movements of his Sonata No. 8 in C Minor (the "Pathétique"), as well as the earlier Sonata in C Minor, Op. 10, No. 1, appear to have served some inspirational purpose. All three share the same key, as well as an atmosphere of prayerful consolation. But the similarity ends there, as Schubert remains his own man in a work of astonishing originality.

The Adagio, an extended ternary form that extends to a somewhat varied repetition of its parts (ABABA) begins optimistically enough. The A section's opening bars are nothing if not a four-part hymn that reprises, with a slight variant, the thematic contour of the first movement's second subject. Migrating in conjunct motion from its tonic, A-flat major, to a definitive cadence on the dominant in the fourth bar of its initial four-bar phrase period, it offers a tranquil vision of an unattainable paradise. The insertion of a secondary dominant in the third bar, duly highlighted by an E-natural on the second beat and its resolution onto an F-minor chord on the third, colors the prevailing harmony with its shadowy concern and somewhat destabilizing presence. The ensuing four-bar consequent, drawn from the dominant of the dominant, reassures its antecedent with a string of descending minor thirds atop the bass's counterpoint in contrary motion. The first two bars of the opening theme are repeated, though now the bass voices are brought northward to the piano's tenor register.

What follows is no anomaly, but a crucial constituent—a prime tenant, if you will—of the Adagio's overall structure. In these two bars, a passage that Fisk dubs the work's focal progression, the harmony, touching on D-flat major, is enriched in a parade of derived dominant and subdominant chords modified by a hairpin crescendo and decrescendo (which, significantly, is a dynamic marking that in Schubert's day usually referred to something other than getting louder or softer; it was also an indication to the performer to slacken the tempo ever so slightly in order to emphasize the affect). The penultimate, minor subdominant chord of the second bar is especially resonant, in that the B-double-flat embedded within it gives off the fragrance of Schubert's old but anxious friend the augmented sixth. What's more, this progression is a throwback to a phrase from yet another *Winterreise* lied, "Gefror'ne Tränen" (Frozen Tears), which shares with it a harmonic and gestural camaraderie. In that song, Schubert again extols the heartbreak of the cycles' itinerant protagonist, or wanderer. Indeed, this two-bar progression can be viewed, when considered in the context of the song's text, as a weeping motive.

The progression is extended further by a fermata placed shrewdly atop its final chord, a D-flat triad on the third beat of its second bar. As if to shake off the figure as a bad omen, the following two measures restore A-flat major before restating Fisk's focal progression, its chords now thickened and elevated to a higher register. The consequent cadence leads inexorably to the murky beginning of the B section, a plaintive lament in D-flat minor that vaguely mimics the melodic design of the opening. Its mournful, chromatically inflected melody, animated by a double dotted rhythm in its second, hollows into a descending pattern in octaves built atop an A-flat-major triad. It hovers over a rotation of sixteenth-notes in the bass en route to a double bar line where the key signature has been obliterated.

But here, Schubert's strategy is no different than it was at a similar spot in the development of the first movement; the absence of flat signs in the signature fails to translate into what it normally would, namely, C major or A minor. Instead, Schubert opens up the harmonic landscape, expanding the theme in the warm embrace of E major. But then, moments later, all hell breaks loose in a terrifying processional. It begins quietly with an urgent pulsation of triplets, which swell quietly in double notes in the bass, while the right hand again gives voice to the double dotted tag that the lament articulated so persuasively. Tensions increase soon, as brusque sforzandos modify double dotted octaves, adroitly placed on the downbeat of each of the next four bars. Evolving from this is a sequence of ascending and descending octaves, likewise configured in triplets and chromatically modulated en route to their high point.

A cadence a few bars later in A-flat establishes anew the serenity of the opening, though not without agitation; this time the left hand is entrusted with a variant of its old flame, offering its lively accompaniment in triplets. On the heels of the third appearance of the focused progression, Schubert lifts the music, transposing the music a half-step higher to A major. With this, a variant of the B section materializes in D minor, though here the urbane placidity of the sixteenth-note rotation in its earlier incarnation is replaced by a steady deliberation of triplets. Soon enough, the key shifts to E-flat minor as the right hand assumes the triplets, converting them from single notes to staccato octaves, while just below, the left hand sings out the lonely lament in a robust *forte*.

But the left hand demands dominion of the triplet figure and retakes it while an expressive progression of widely spaced chords struts above. Without warning, the modality shifts to F major as the dynamic diminishes to a *subito piano* and the double dotted lament returns astride a nervous sheen of thirty-second-notes. The ominous triplets and octave sforzandos move in again, like cumulus clouds about to break into storm, preparing the way for the third and final reinstatement of the A section.

Here, the principal subject, its hymnlike character preserved, spreads out into widely spaced chords. Schubert enlists and reinvents motivic and rhythmic ideas culled from the previous sections, though now refashioned to coincide with the hymn. Thus the sixteenth-note rotations that first emerged in the initial presentation of the second subject morph into a breathy accompaniment. Some eight bars later, a brief descent in triplets in the melody suggests that neither regret nor the allusion to it has been left behind. The ever-present focused progression emerges again, moving upward in chromatic increments from C major to D major. The melancholy consequent again yields to a dominant seventh of A major, but following a rest it breathes its last only moments later when it is repeated a semitone lower, in the tonic, A-flat major.

The net effect of this chromatic shift downward in concert with the reiteration of this melancholy figure is suggestive: of regret, loneliness, faded memory, and resignation. Indeed, the chromatic juxtaposition of A major and A-flat major is in itself a metaphor for alienation that telegraphs a familiar sentiment: so near, and yet so far. The final four bars draw the Adagio to a close on a note of pious yearning as a pair of fluid triplets rise to a high E-flat, only to descend to the tonic moments later. The immanent conflict posed by the chromatic juxtaposition of these keys evokes the serene quiescence of an earlier time, both metaphorically and in compositional categories. The work draws to its quiet conclusion on three A-flat-major triads.

Third movement: Menuetto—Allegro

The serpentine opening theme of this disarming Menuetto owes a debt of gratitude to the tune that spawned it, namely, the second subject of the first movement. Restoring this movement to the sonata's principal key, C minor, the Menuetto begins gracefully, albeit with an air of consternation; it proceeds with a stepwise ascent in quarter-note octaves that likewise land on an octave on G-natural just over the bar line. Under a slur, the G slides up by a half-step to A-flat on the third beat. Below, an Alberti bass rumbles quietly, its patter of running eighth-notes providing shelter to two voices rather than one, despite the notation that might suggest otherwise. The opening twelve-bar phrase divides asymmetrically into three parts, the second of which picks up steam in the fourth bar as it continues to ascend, through A-flat major, to F minor, and then to its reassuring final consequent, which boasts adjacent tonic and dominant chords in E-flat major.

A lively upbeat introduces the B section. It is a bold arpeggiation of four notes in E-flat major that alights proudly on two E-flat triads successively spread out over the ensuing bar. In between these chordal profusions, Schubert inserts eighth-note arpeggiations, likewise giving resonance, within its first six bars, to an E-flat-major triad. Meanwhile the chordal figures, the first beats of which are each modified by a hearty sforzando, segue into a C-minor arpeggiation, but only briefly. A measure later, A-flat major negates it's the C-minor figure's impact and moves swiftly into two insistent bars of repeated and unharmonized

A-flats in unison. These powerful pitches, modified by a crescendo, move with forthright dispatch into a diminished seventh chord that holds its own until resolving back to A-flat one bar later. The inclusion in this chord of an F-flat suggests a Neapolitan relation; certainly, whatever the color it imparts, a subjective, extramusical interpretation might say its presence is menacing. It is most certainly disruptive: to the prevailing harmony, to the lean overall texture, and last but not least, to the rhythm, which, though it never stops, momentarily coalesces in this one sonority.

A cadence on C minor's dominant ushers in the second phase of the material. Here, the right hand assumes a fanciful variant of the principal theme, which is now elaborated as a string of purring eighth-notes. At the same time, the left hand likewise articulates the principal melody, preserving its rhythmic contours but compressing it into closed triads. An unexpected rest brings things to a sudden halt, without explanation; it is a philosophical pause into which the previous material dissolves. But the figuration resumes in inversion as the left hand serves up the principal theme, still configured in closely knit triads but now recast in A-flat major. Four bars later, another rest interrupts the proceedings as the figure cadences in F minor, C minor's subdominant. The four bars that conclude the B section, though configured in the same manner as that which preceded them, are distinguished by a pair of discreet accents, which Schubert places lightly atop two pitches, A-flat and E-flat, in the adjoining middle bars of the phrase. Though the harmonic countenance of these measures sidles clearly to C minor, these notes, when slightly accentuated, radiate just enough of A-flat major to leave a ghostly imprimatur of the now passé subdominant of E-flat major.

Six beats, not bars, of silence precede the trio. Its entry on an upbeat—a single C-natural—sets forth its slim, three-voiced texture, which is adroitly led by a suave, roly-poly melody in the right hand's alto voice. Its lilting rhythm, though conventional for its Viennese leanings, stays afloat on the crest of its four-bar phrase periods. The Trio's B section likewise conforms to the convention, but for that it loses not an iota of charm. Here its carefree theme shifts into a higher register in E-flat major. Only four bars later, a prolonged G-flat in the tenor register welcomes E-flat minor as its temporary key center. A playful splash of rising and falling eighth-notes, carried in the right hand across the alto register, lends its support to a melodic fragment just north of it. The intermittent, off-beat punctuations of the bass propel the phrase forward into a brief trochaic recall of the Menuetto's second phase.

With the return of the Menuetto, now played without repeats, this disarming third movement concludes as quietly as it began.

Fourth movement: Allegro

The driving howl that informs this spirited tarantella in rondo sonata form extols obsession as an aesthetic objective in its own right. An old and entirely apocryphal myth holds that the tarantella owes its name to a hairy, long-limbed arachnid, or to the cure surrounding its venomous bite. The tarantella is actually a folk dance indigenous to southern Italy, where it inherited its name from the village of Taranto. It is distinguished by its swift tempo in 6/8 time and by its rapid shifts of modality from major to minor.

Even so, the old myth, no matter how false, has a certain resonance in this supercharged Schubertian finale, which is likewise an evocation of death and perhaps the madness that, in Schubert's day, was associated with infectious disease. But to characterize this movement as merely an attempt to codify some ersatz image of death, or the image repertoire that surrounds death, would not only do the work a disservice, but would be an oversimplification. While it contains an abundance of references to the sonata's previous movements, and thus to motivic material inspired by the fatalistic songs of *Winterreise*, it is not wholly dependent on either. Indeed, though incontrovertibly a part of the sonata as a whole, its compositional structure unfolds with evolutionary fervor, as if evolution itself could be accelerated and experienced within the space of a few minutes. From its highly idiosyncratic and easily identifiable parts springs a sum that is greater than any one of them. Whether that sum can be interpreted as its composer's vision of death, and particularly his own imminent demise, is a speculative exercise.

And yet, given the circumstances of Schubert's failing health, as well as the proximity of this composition to the ever-so-philosophical dimensions of *Winterreise* (and *Schwanengesang*), it is hardly implausible that death, and what came after, was very much on his mind. If he was indeed determined, in some wholly private way (and he was a timorous individual who never took much pleasure in public situations), to express his fear or even his longing for death in compositional categories, and if that determination informed his musical gestuary and ideational substance, then we are all the richer for it. In the end, I'm not sure it really matters; what his own music meant to him and what it means to individual listeners two hundred years later are not mutually exclusive. In the final analysis, music means different things to different people— for different reasons. We get out of it only as much as we put in.

But no one is a mind reader. Thus the work itself must be counted on to yield its treasure of hidden forces, hushed intimacies, and provocative secrets. Whatever it might suggest, if not definitively state (which, in music, is a logical impossibility), about Schubert's psychological disposition, or about the human condition, for that matter, is something that listeners have to determine for themselves. In the meantime, rather than second-guess anyone's intentions, let's have a look at this stunning movement.

The thematic whirlwind that gives way to the first eight-bar phrase period exemplifies musical intensity in any number of ways. First off, there is a persistent rhythm, configured as an orgy of successive iambs in the right hand, which rides astride a continual pulsation, in the left, of six eighth-notes to the bar. The texture is surprisingly lean; only two voices, the bass and treble, constitute the first ninety measures. Even so, the mood remains tense as the metrical organization winds each and every one of its many notes into a tightly wound coil, ready to break at any moment.

The principal theme itself proceeds largely in a parade of two-note iambs in disjunct motion, though an ascending minor sixth, followed by a descending stepwise sprint, inaugurates it. Soon enough, the breathless, upbeat character implied in virtually every one of these two-note cells leads, in conventional fashion, to a strongly accented dominant that is too busy to cadence normally. In this work, there is no rest for the weary. Though the second phrase period mimics the first, it parts ways with its comrade with a sturdy announcement of the tonic on two

C-naturals, which bellow forth at the distance of a three-octave span. The pitch rises in ascending chromatic sequences, which soon debouche into D-flat major and a voluptuous spread of the two-note cells, now configured in leaping octaves.

A sarcastic southward gallop ensues in the soprano register as both modality and key centers migrate instantaneously from D-flat major to D-flat minor, C minor, and, after the dissolution of the key signature a few bars later, C major. Maintaining without interruption the motivic figuration established by the principal subject, the music segues, with minimal preparation—which amounts to the profuse repetition of a D-flat and an A-flat skillfully and repeatedly embedded in a mélange of C major, F minor, and diminished arpeggiations—into the second subject. A single D-flat, prolonged *fortissimo* by an octave doubling over two entire bars, demarcates the entry of this energetic new figure. It is cleanly defined by a vigorous ascending scale that pushes its way, astride a string of dominant sevenths, up to the same pitch, now remanded to the registrational stratosphere. On its heels is a brief consequent, a thickly configured dominant triad that, while appropriating the iamb, is effectively a dotted rhythm. This forceful event is nothing less than a recall of the first movement's opening tag. Just in case anyone should forget, a sequence of tonic, that is, D-flat major, chords take charge, hurling themselves from the upper to the lower registers amid periodic quarter-rest punctuations.

True to form, Schubert introduces yet a third subject to this busy exposition. A shift to C-sharp minor serves the quiet imposition of a new motive: a sequence of falling fifths, which pass from treble to bass in a virtuosic exchange. Indeed, it is a passage that requires from the pianist considerable physical agility and interpretive savoir-faire. This in turn compels me to digress, for a moment, to a subject that I explore in greater depth in my book on Liszt and that deserves at least honorable mention in this volume.

No one should underestimate the power of affective conveyance by means of virtuosity, even in music so substantive and exalted as to be as pure as the driven snow. Without question, the harrowing intensity that informs so much of this startling tarantella is a consequence of its compositional organization. Pianists face a difficult job, in that they are obliged to identify, without rewriting, the music's salient points as they elaborates its rich fabric of motivic signifiers. The manner in which they adjudicate so much acoustic information will depend largely on their understanding of form, content, and harmonic orientation, as well as the disposition of its complex rhythms. All of these will in turn inform their physical approach to the realization of concrete musical goals; the strategy for interpretation and execution must be at least equal to the composer's compositional aesthetic objectives. If it is not, pianists will fail to deliver anything other than a musical skeleton, entirely shorn of substance.

Certainly, in the best possible world, pianists who have cultivated a comprehensive listening apparatus will put their skills to work in the service of musical values. In such gifted hands, music becomes a multidimensional experience that not only unfolds in time, but also evolves into a luxurious network of distinctive sonorities piquantly articulated for their harmonic function and rhythmic nuance. Absent such a depth of musical understanding—that is, a firm grasp of how a composition and the myriad motivic motors that drive it are put together, and what's more, how they *work* together—virtuosity yields nothing; it is an empty vessel. But when virtuosity is fueled by authentic curiosity and insight; when it takes delight in harmonic conflict and rhythmic differentiation; and when it is given to affectively highlighting these and other significant compositional features, that is when virtuosity gains both prestige and credibility.

Thus the thrill of seeing as well as hearing pianists engage in the tight-rope act of rapid hand crossing, all the while making sense of the music under their fingers, is hardly detrimental to musical experience, but a contributing factor. Rather than spend too much time here on this important and sometimes taboo subject (in the hallowed halls of academia), I prefer to cite the celebrated French philosopher and aesthetician Vladimir Jankélévitch:

> Virtuosity does not exist on credit; there is no such thing as a virtuoso in whom one can have confidence simply because of his good intentions. . . . One cannot believe in a virtuoso based on what he says; one can only recognize his acts, his manner of *doing*. Don't listen to what a virtuoso says, but listen to what he *does*.

> The sincerity of a virtuoso is recognizable only in an effective
> performance, and not through a dissertation about the concept of
> performance. . . . Virtuosity presumes not only an aptitude, but
> also the exercise of that aptitude; it is neither a quiescent memory,
> nor a promise, nor a *fait accompli*, nor a platonic virtue, but is
> instead the fullness of accomplishment. As Aristotle put it: That
> which virtuosity does is not only about capacity, it is about *energy*,
> that is, the power of activity. And not only energy, but *entelechy*,
> that is, the energy that actualizes success. Nothing matters but
> success! Virtuosity is judged mercilessly on the results. [Vladimir
> Jankélévitch: *Liszt et la rhapsodie: Un essai sur la virtuosité*, Paris:
> Edition Plon, 1978, this translation by John Bell Young]

And so it is with this technically and interpretively treacherous
finale, which demands a comprehensive grasp of its many parts if it
is to be successfully conveyed. Nowhere is that more relevant than in
the aforementioned passage, namely, the third subject whose analysis I
briefly set aside in favor of a discussion of virtuosity.

Amplifying the second subject's jocular panorama of jumping fifths
is a well-compacted chromatic scale that angles downward and up again
in the soprano voice over two bars. This it does three times, recalling
the willowy chromatic scales that drew the first movement's development to a close. New opportunities for crossing the hands arise when
Schubert combines a variant of these truncated scales with the bouncing fifths. The mood remains relatively playful until a change of key to
E-flat minor gathers the force of the iambs in massively expanded minor
chords. As if an antidote to the motivic imperialism of the descending
scale in the opening bars of the first movement, an ascending run carries the day in unison to a nervous variant of these thematic fragments.
Just as suddenly, the dynamic dwindles to *pianissimo*, welcoming a
new melodic idea in E-flat major. It introduces itself as a benign and
unruffled presence of lyrical octaves articulated over a pattern of three
eighths—half the value of the 6/8 bar—and a dotted quarter, which
completes that value.

Following a cadence on the dominant of E-flat, and two full bars of
silence, Schubert satisfies the work's aesthetic movement with the inclusion of an exceptionally engaging tune, drawn in part from the scalar

and intervallic figures of the previous section. It alights in B major with all the grace of a forest butterfly, its delicate wings aflutter in a sylvan and often mercurial dance. The sudden shift from E-flat major to B major startles for the cold but ever-so-refreshing wind it blows across the tonal landscape; what it evokes, though only metaphor, borders on a meteorological phenomenon, such as those rare but crystalline autumn days in New England when summer, shocked out of its languid sobriety, suddenly turns into fall. Its character is gossamer as it spins itself out across the gentle, evenhanded, and unobtrusive rivulets of eighth-notes in the bass.

That B major tune can also be interpreted as C-flat major, given the movement's harmonic history and teleology, providing no end of enticement for scholars and interpreters, but this will matter not at all to the average listener, nor should it. This is, after all, the movement's development, although it is so only by proxy and because conventional analysis requires nomination of some sort or another. Strictly speaking, the tune is a new rather than an old melodic idea. Therefore, its role is assured within the sonata's compositional diaspora, and whatever happens to it from here on in will serve only to enrich the musical texture. That alone should be enough to accord it the moniker of development.

Having made its case in a twelve-bar phrase period, the tune dissolves into a lean descending scale, a fragment of its elegant melisma materializes in the piano's tenor voice and is reiterated in sequence beneath a playful parade of iambic broken octaves. Key centers migrate quickly and perceptibly here, moving steadily from E minor, to D minor, and then to C minor. Traces of the Adagio's central harmonic escapade inform the texture here, as the left hand engages a rotation of successive major and minor sixths.

A new, perhaps more optimistic, period begins, extending itself into considerably longer phrase units and briefly favoring major modalities. The mood has turned bright, even joyous, as if the vision of paradise is attainable. Torrents of arpeggios and scales, deftly harmonized below, yield to a fairly rapid harmonic rhythm, having gained visitation rights to D-flat major, A-flat major and E-flat major. The texture swells with a march of weighty octaves evenly distributed, two per bar, in the bass against a storm of blustery ascending scales in the right. A G-major scale, standing alone and unaccompanied, falls precipitously into a D-flat-minor triad before making its way to the dominant of C minor in preparation for the recapitulation.

Following a more-or-less verbatim reiteration of the exposition, the coda commences with a harmonic progression identical to the opening bars of the first movement, albeit substantially expanded and rhythmically configured to accommodate the iambs. A pulsation of open fifths in the bass, like so many bagpipes, informs the coda's first eight bars and then returns, after an alteration, for another eight. A fermata draws the first part of the coda into the second, which regurgitates the materials of the movement's first page. The iambs approach their final descent, first in D-flat, and then, en route to the finish line, C minor. Some twenty-five bars before the end, two pitches, D-flat and D-natural, compete for supremacy as the iambic figure intensifies, first in alternating patterns of ascent and descent. But neither pitch, for all the tension created, is a match for the omnipotent power of the tonic, which puts its solemn foot down for the final thirteen. Two powerful chords, dominant and tonic, draw the work to its definitive and ever-so-grave conclusion.

The finality of this finale is itself a metaphor for its composer's tragically premature demise. If it is a dance of death, which common sense, if not an objective analysis, suggests, then it is certainly Schubert's own. Though it could be interpreted, on some metamusical and even uncontextualized level, as both a maelstrom of anxiety and a vision of paradise, it is also Schubert's other *Schwanengesang*—his swan song. In combination with the two other sonatas, in A major and in B-flat major, which together give shape to a musico-aesthetic trilogy, it becomes something greater than the sum of its many parts. It is not merely a highly personal vision of death, which would be an oversimplification and unworthy of Schubert's genius, but a vision of the future of musical composition itself. For their originality, breathtaking harmonic invention, and cyclical themes that reinvent musical allusion as a legitimate compositional strategy, each of these works broke important new ground. But in the final analysis, the real credit for breaking new ground must go to the man himself, Franz Schubert, whose abundant gifts to art and civilization have proved as poignant as they are immeasurable.

Glossary

accelerando   A gradual heightening or cumulative quickening of tempo.

adagio   A slow tempo, but neither turgid nor comatose. An adagio must move, broadly.

affect   Comes from the *Affektenlehre*, or Doctrine of Affects, a seventeenth-century aesthetic ideology that the emotions could be codified in sound and that a rhetorical grammar of such affections could be made part of compositional procedure. Though not exactly interchangeable with our use of the term, it is a species of inflection and is best described as referring to the degree of emphasis, dynamic weight, or perspective performers invest in any given motivic figuration.

allegretto   A lively, quick, and above all playful tempo, but not quite so fast as allegro.

allegro   Generally understood to be a fast or moderately fast tempo, but in music of the baroque and classical eras, especially, it refers to character and disposition; it can be construed to mean cheerful or happy.

anapest   A poetic foot of three syllables, two short followed by one long in quantitative meter, and two unstressed followed by one stressed in accentual meter.

andante   A gracious, walking tempo, not too slow nor too quick. Subject to any number of gradations.

articulation	The manner in which a performer distinguishes (by means of attack, prolongation, and release) certain tones, motives, phrases, and groups of pitches individually and in relation to each other. Composers either spell out or provide symbols to indicate types of articulation, such as staccato, legato, wedges, tenuto, and other accent marks.
baroque music	Music composed between roughly 1590 and 1750 that embraces certain styles and techniques attributable to the aesthetic ideas, formulations, and philosophy of the era. Due to its long run, it is usually divided into three distinct subperiods of its own, each governed by specific innovations. Opera, the fugue, and the harmonization of a ground bass were products of baroque invention.
cadence	A harmonic progression that demarcates the end of a phrase or larger section of a work and provides a sense of resolution, with varying degrees of finality. In its harmonic tendency to move back toward the key of the work, cadence is also an expression of a composition's tonality.
cadenza	An extended solo passage usually, but not only, found in a concerto. It typically comes toward the end of a concerto or sonata form movement, before the coda, and it elaborates and ornaments the principal themes of the work with a view toward showing off the skill of its composer or soloist, or both. Though composers sometimes write out the cadenza, performers, too, occasionally write their own.
canon	A musical pattern defined by a thematic subject that is presented, then successively imitated, by one or more voices commencing on different pitches. There are different kinds of canon: fixed, which

is imitation by rote; and free, which introduces modifications of pitch material and rhythm.

classical era The period of musical composition that extended from the early eighteenth through the early nineteenth century. Its exact division into years is difficult to measure, as classicism evolved slowly, and its attendant techniques and aesthetics eventually bled into romanticism. Characteristics of music of the classical era include periodic phrasing, longer harmonic rhythms, a prevalence of simpler, more natural melodic designs, homophonic textures, and greater use of specifically marked dynamic contrasts.

coda The concluding section of a movement or single composition that usually encapsulates the work's principal themes. A coda may be as brief as a few measures, or elaborate and extensive.

counterpoint The simultaneous unfolding of two or more melodies, and the various compositional principles that govern their existence and formulation—that is, their movement away from each other, their rhythmic differences, and the resultant harmonies they create in relation to each other.

crescendo, decrescendo A gradual, cumulative increase or decrease in volume indicated by hairpin signs or written out by the composer. This intensification of sound in either direction informs the affective character of the passage it modifies.

cretic A poetic foot, composed of one short syllable between two long ones.

cyclic form A technique of musical construction, involving multiple sections or movements, in which a theme, melody, or thematic material occurs in more than one movement as a unifying device.

dactyl	A poetic foot of three syllables, one long followed by two short, or one stressed followed by two unstressed.
development	The middle section of a movement in sonata form, wherein the principal themes and motivic ideas are varied, elaborated, intensified, and ornamented, en route to the recapitulation.
dominant	Every major and minor scale consists of seven pitches; the fifth degree of the scale is called the dominant. A chord constructed around this pitch includes the seventh degree of the scale. The tendency of the seventh degree to move toward its neighboring tonic pitch is strong and creates a feeling of expectation and desire for resolution in its listeners.
diminution	The presentation of a melody in note values shorter than those in which it was originally cast.
dotted note	A dot placed just alongside a pitch that increases the temporal value of that note by one-half of its original value. Two dots set in this way increase the value by yet another quarter of that value.
exposition	The first section of a sonata, in which the principal themes of the compositions are presented in juxtaposition one to the other, and including at least one major modulation to a secondary key, most often, but not necessarily, the dominant.
French sixth	A chord with the tones flat-6, 1, 2, sharp-4; in C major, it would be spelled A-flat–C–D–F-sharp. Called "French" because its notes are all contained within the same whole-tone scale, lending a sonority common in French music in the nineteenth century.
fugue	A composition in which a theme (also known as a subject) is stated and then repeated consecutively in two or more voices in imitative counterpoint. This confluence of voices is then elaborated, extended,

varied, modulated, and developed in any number of ways.

fugato   A usually brief contrapuntal section that occurs within a sonata movement or other form and that, while at once contrapuntal and imitative—the essential elements of a fugue—does not develop into a full-blown fugue.

hemiola   A kind of rhythmic substitute, wherein two measures in triple meter are both notated and played in the same temporal space as three bars in duple meter.

mediant   Refers to a pitch, chord, or tonality based on the third degree of a major or minor scale.

menuetto (minuet)   An elegant dance in 3/4 time that had its origins in seventeenth-century France. Usually in two-part (binary) form, with its second beats often accented. When danced, the minuet was a little slower than when performed strictly as instrumental music.

motive, motif   A brief rhythmic unit of a specific duration and design that attains to its own identity and becomes the basis of more elaborate structures, movements, and whole works.

Neapolitan sixth   A chromatically inflected inverted triad (that is, one with the third at the bottom rather than in the middle) that is based on the lowered second degree of the scale; it can be major or minor. In C major, the Neapolitan sixth is based on D-flat, with F natural as the lowest pitch.

pedal point   A single tone, reiterated and sustained under changing harmonic patterns and over an extended period. While pedal points frequently occur in the bass, they can also be dispatched in any voice to enhance harmonic and rhythmic tension.

piano; pianissimo   Soft; very soft.

pizzicato   For stringed instruments, an articulation wherein the string is plucked with the fingers rather than bowed.

polyphony   Wherein several musical voices, or lines, are heard in combination, and where each line has an independent character.

recapitulation   In sonata form, the concluding section of a movement wherein all the principal themes of the work are restated, usually in the tonic key.

scherzo   A light, playful, even mischievous dance form that, in the late eighteenth century and nineteenth century, often replaced the minuet as a movement in symphonies and in instrumental music. It is played swiftly in 3/4 time and includes a contrasting trio section.

sforzando   A sudden, interruptive accentuation.

sonata form   The traditional form used most often in the first movements of instrumental music from the classical period and beyond. Though it can be identified by a few standard organizational procedures—exposition, development, and recapitulation, as well as key relationships that juxtapose tonic and dominant in the first section, and so on—it is best viewed as a dynamic process.

staccato   The distinct separation of the pitch from its neighboring notes. From the baroque era onward, staccato was an articulation marking, indicated by a dot above the note that instructed the player to cancel the prevailing legato.

subdominant   Refers to a pitch, chord, or tonality based on the fourth degree of a major or minor scale.

submediant	Refers to a pitch, chord, or tonality based on the sixth degree of a major or minor scale.
syncope (short for syncopation)	A temporary shift of accentuation that contradicts the metrical organization within a bar or phrase, though the metrical identity of the passage stays intact. For example, an accent on a weak beat of a bar on the heels of unaccented strong beat will modify the function of those beats, turning a weak beat into a strong beat, and can thus affect harmonic orientation, articulation, and rhythmic trajectory.
tempo	The rate of speed at which a piece of music is played; a specific tempo is indicated by composers, who rely on performers to respect their instructions according to the universally understood precepts and in accordance with contemporary performance practice.
thematic transformation	A compositional process whereby a theme is altered, manipulated, and varied in such a way as to maintain its identity yet change its immanent character.
tonality	The organization of tones around a single central pitch, or tonic. Tonality comprises all twelve major and minor keys, as well as the scales, triads, and harmonic functions that define them.
tremolo	The rapid repetition of a single pitch or chord. Used for purposes of affective and dramatic intensification.
triplet	Three notes of equal value played in place of two notes of equal value.

CD Track Listing

1. Symphony No. 8 in B minor, D. 759 ("Unfinished"): First
   Movement—Allegro moderato (12:00)
   Wilhelm Furtwängler, conductor, Berlin Philharmonic
   Ⓟ 2008 Music & Arts Programs of America, Inc. Courtesy of Music & Arts.
   From Music & Arts CD 1218

2. Fantasia in C major, D. 760 ("Wanderer"): Allegro con fuoco ma
   non troppo (6:37)
   Paul Badura-Skoda, piano
   Ⓟ 2009 Music & Arts Programs of America, Inc. Courtesy of Music & Arts.
   From Music & Arts CD 4267

3. Fantasia in C major, D. 760 ("Wanderer"): Adagio (6:28)
   Paul Badura-Skoda, piano
   Ⓟ 2009 Music & Arts Programs of America, Inc. Courtesy of Music & Arts.
   From Music & Arts CD 4267

4. Fantasia in C major, D. 760 ("Wanderer"): Allegro (3:53)
   Paul Badura-Skoda, piano
   Ⓟ 2009 Music & Arts Programs of America, Inc. Courtesy of Music & Arts.
   From Music & Arts CD 4267

5. Impromptu Op. 90 No. 1 in C minor, D. 899 (10:25)
   Juana Zayas, piano
   Ⓟ 2009 Music & Arts Programs of America, Inc. Courtesy of Music & Arts.
   From Music & Arts CD 1139

6. Impromptu Op. 90 No. 3 in E-flat major, D. 899 (4:49)

    Juana Zayas, piano

    Ⓟ 2009 Music & Arts Programs of America, Inc. Courtesy of Music & Arts.
    From Music & Arts CD 1139

7. Impromptu Op. 90 No. 2 in G-flat major, D. 899 (6:00)

    Juana Zayas, piano

    Ⓟ 2009 Music & Arts Programs of America, Inc. Courtesy of Music & Arts.
    From Music & Arts CD 1139

8. Impromptu Op. 90 No. 4 in A-flat major, D. 899 (7:55)

    Juana Zayas, piano

    Ⓟ 2009 Music & Arts Programs of America, Inc. Courtesy of Music & Arts.
    From Music & Arts CD 1139

9. Quintet in C major, D. 956: Adagio (12:22)

    Jacob Krachmalnik, violin; Aurel Pernea, violin; Karen Tuttle, viola;
    Madeline Foley, cello; and Pablo Casals, cello

    Ⓟ 2009 Music & Arts Programs of America, Inc. Courtesy of Music & Arts.
    From Music & Arts CD 1113